Mometrix
TEST PREPARATION

I0878888

Florida

Grade 3 ELA Reading Test Prep Workbook

DEAR FUTURE EXAM SUCCESS STORY

First of all, **THANK YOU** for purchasing Mometrix study materials!

Second, congratulations! You are one of the few determined test-takers who are committed to doing whatever it takes to excel on your exam. **You have come to the right place.** We developed these study materials with one goal in mind: to deliver you the information you need in a format that's concise and easy to use.

In addition to optimizing your guide for the content of the test, we've outlined our recommended steps for breaking down the preparation process into small, attainable goals so you can make sure you stay on track.

We've also analyzed the entire test-taking process, identifying the most common pitfalls and showing how you can overcome them and be ready for any curveball the test throws you.

Standardized testing is one of the biggest obstacles on your road to success, which only increases the importance of doing well in the high-pressure, high-stakes environment of test day. Your results on this test could have a significant impact on your future, and this guide provides the information and practical advice to help you achieve your full potential on test day.

Your success is our success

We would love to hear from you! If you would like to share the story of your exam success or if you have any questions or comments in regard to our products, please contact us at **800-673-8175** or **support@mometrix.com**.

Thanks again for your business and we wish you continued success!

Sincerely,
The Mometrix Test Preparation Team

Written and edited by the Mometrix Exam Secrets Test Prep Team
Printed in the United States of America

TABLE OF CONTENTS

Introduction

Thank you for purchasing this resource! You have made the choice to prepare yourself for a test that could have a huge impact on your future, and this guide is designed to help you be fully ready for test day. Obviously, it's important to have a solid understanding of the test material, but you also need to be prepared for the unique environment and stressors of the test, so that you can perform to the best of your abilities.

For this purpose, the first section that appears in this guide is the **Secret Keys**. We've devoted countless hours to meticulously researching what works and what doesn't, and we've boiled down our findings to the five most impactful steps you can take to improve your performance on the test. We start at the beginning with study planning and move through the preparation process, all the way to the testing strategies that will help you get the most out of what you know when you're finally sitting in front of the test.

We recommend that you start preparing for your test as far in advance as possible. However, if you've bought this guide as a last-minute study resource and only have a few days before your test, we recommend that you skip over the first two Secret Keys since they address a long-term study plan.

If you struggle with **test anxiety**, we strongly encourage you to check out our recommendations for how you can overcome it. Test anxiety is a formidable foe, but it can be beaten, and we want to make sure you have the tools you need to defeat it.

Secret Key #1 – Plan Big, Study Small

There's a lot riding on your performance. If you want to ace this test, you're going to need to keep your skills sharp and the material fresh in your mind. You need a plan that lets you review everything you need to know while still fitting in your schedule. We'll break this strategy down into three categories.

Information Organization

Start with the information you already have: the official test outline. From this, you can make a complete list of all the concepts you need to cover before the test. Organize these concepts into groups that can be studied together, and create a list of any related vocabulary you need to learn so you can brush up on any difficult terms. You'll want to keep this vocabulary list handy once you actually start studying since you may need to add to it along the way.

Time Management

Once you have your set of study concepts, decide how to spread them out over the time you have left before the test. Break your study plan into small, clear goals so you have a manageable task for each day and know exactly what you're doing. Then just focus on one small step at a time. When you manage your time this way, you don't need to spend hours at a time studying. Studying a small block of content for a short period each day helps you retain information better and avoid stressing over how much you have left to do. You can relax knowing that you have a plan to cover everything in time. In order for this strategy to be effective though, you have to start studying early and stick to your schedule. Avoid the exhaustion and futility that comes from last-minute cramming!

Study Environment

The environment you study in has a big impact on your learning. Studying in a coffee shop, while probably more enjoyable, is not likely to be as fruitful as studying in a quiet room. It's important to keep distractions to a minimum. You're only planning to study for a short block of time, so make the most of it. Don't pause to check your phone or get up to find a snack. It's also important to **avoid multitasking**. Research has consistently shown that multitasking will make your studying dramatically less effective. Your study area should also be comfortable and well-lit so you don't have the distraction of straining your eyes or sitting on an uncomfortable chair.

The time of day you study is also important. You want to be rested and alert. Don't wait until just before bedtime. Study when you'll be most likely to comprehend and remember. Even better, if you know what time of day your test will be, set that time aside for study. That way your brain will be used to working on that subject at that specific time and you'll have a better chance of recalling information.

Finally, it can be helpful to team up with others who are studying for the same test. Your actual studying should be done in as isolated an environment as possible, but the work of organizing the information and setting up the study plan can be divided up. In between study sessions, you can discuss with your teammates the concepts that you're all studying and quiz each other on the details. Just be sure that your teammates are as serious about the test as you are. If you find that your study time is being replaced with social time, you might need to find a new team.

Secret Key #2 – Make Your Studying Count

You're devoting a lot of time and effort to preparing for this test, so you want to be absolutely certain it will pay off. This means doing more than just reading the content and hoping you can remember it on test day. It's important to make every minute of study count. There are two main areas you can focus on to make your studying count.

Retention

It doesn't matter how much time you study if you can't remember the material. You need to make sure you are retaining the concepts. To check your retention of the information you're learning, try recalling it at later times with minimal prompting. Try carrying around flashcards and glance at one or two from time to time or ask a friend who's also studying for the test to quiz you.

To enhance your retention, look for ways to put the information into practice so that you can apply it rather than simply recalling it. If you're using the information in practical ways, it will be much easier to remember. Similarly, it helps to solidify a concept in your mind if you're not only reading it to yourself but also explaining it to someone else. Ask a friend to let you teach them about a concept you're a little shaky on (or speak aloud to an imaginary audience if necessary). As you try to summarize, define, give examples, and answer your friend's questions, you'll understand the concepts better and they will stay with you longer. Finally, step back for a big picture view and ask yourself how each piece of information fits with the whole subject. When you link the different concepts together and see them working together as a whole, it's easier to remember the individual components.

Finally, practice showing your work on any multi-step problems, even if you're just studying. Writing out each step you take to solve a problem will help solidify the process in your mind, and you'll be more likely to remember it during the test.

Modality

Modality simply refers to the means or method by which you study. Choosing a study modality that fits your own individual learning style is crucial. No two people learn best in exactly the same way, so it's important to know your strengths and use them to your advantage.

For example, if you learn best by visualization, focus on visualizing a concept in your mind and draw an image or a diagram. Try color-coding your notes, illustrating them, or creating symbols that will trigger your mind to recall a learned concept. If you learn best by hearing or discussing information, find a study partner who learns the same way or read aloud to yourself. Think about how to put the information in your own words. Imagine that you are giving a lecture on the topic and record yourself so you can listen to it later.

For any learning style, flashcards can be helpful. Organize the information so you can take advantage of spare moments to review. Underline key words or phrases. Use different colors for different categories. Mnemonic devices (such as creating a short list in which every item starts with the same letter) can also help with retention. Find what works best for you and use it to store the information in your mind most effectively and easily.

Secret Key #3 – Practice the Right Way

Your success on test day depends not only on how many hours you put into preparing, but also on whether you prepared the right way. It's good to check along the way to see if your studying is paying off. One of the most effective ways to do this is by taking practice tests to evaluate your progress. Practice tests are useful because they show exactly where you need to improve. Every time you take a practice test, pay special attention to these three groups of questions:

- The questions you got wrong
- The questions you had to guess on, even if you guessed right
- The questions you found difficult or slow to work through

This will show you exactly what your weak areas are, and where you need to devote more study time. Ask yourself why each of these questions gave you trouble. Was it because you didn't understand the material? Was it because you didn't remember the vocabulary? Do you need more repetitions on this type of question to build speed and confidence? Dig into those questions and figure out how you can strengthen your weak areas as you go back to review the material.

Additionally, many practice tests have a section explaining the answer choices. It can be tempting to read the explanation and think that you now have a good understanding of the concept. However, an explanation likely only covers part of the question's broader context. Even if the explanation makes perfect sense, **go back and investigate** every concept related to the question until you're positive you have a thorough understanding.

As you go along, keep in mind that the practice test is just that: practice. Memorizing these questions and answers will not be very helpful on the actual test because it is unlikely to have any of the same exact questions. If you only know the right answers to the sample questions, you won't be prepared for the real thing. **Study the concepts** until you understand them fully, and then you'll be able to answer any question that shows up on the test.

It's important to wait on the practice tests until you're ready. If you take a test on your first day of study, you may be overwhelmed by the amount of material covered and how much you need to learn. Work up to it gradually.

On test day, you'll need to be prepared for answering questions, managing your time, and using the test-taking strategies you've learned. It's a lot to balance, like a mental marathon that will have a big impact on your future. Like training for a marathon, you'll need to start slowly and work your way up. When test day arrives, you'll be ready.

Start with the strategies you've read in the first two Secret Keys—plan your course and study in the way that works best for you. If you have time, consider using multiple study resources to get different approaches to the same concepts. It can be helpful to see difficult concepts from more than one angle. Then find a good source for practice tests. Many times, the test website will suggest potential study resources or provide sample tests.

Practice Test Strategy

If you're able to find at least three practice tests, we recommend this strategy:

Untimed and Open-Book Practice

Take the first test with no time constraints and with your notes and study guide handy. Take your time and focus on applying the strategies you've learned.

Timed and Open-Book Practice

Take the second practice test open-book as well, but set a timer and practice pacing yourself to finish in time.

Timed and Closed-Book Practice

Take any other practice tests as if it were test day. Set a timer and put away your study materials. Sit at a table or desk in a quiet room, imagine yourself at the testing center, and answer questions as quickly and accurately as possible.

Keep repeating timed and closed-book tests on a regular basis until you run out of practice tests or it's time for the actual test. Your mind will be ready for the schedule and stress of test day, and you'll be able to focus on recalling the material you've learned.

Secret Key #4 – Pace Yourself

Once you're fully prepared for the material on the test, your biggest challenge on test day will be managing your time. Just knowing that the clock is ticking can make you panic even if you have plenty of time left. Work on pacing yourself so you can build confidence against the time constraints of the exam. Pacing is a difficult skill to master, especially in a high-pressure environment, so **practice is vital**.

Set time expectations for your pace based on how much time is available. For example, if a section has 60 questions and the time limit is 30 minutes, you know you have to average 30 seconds or less per question in order to answer them all. Although 30 seconds is the hard limit, set 25 seconds per question as your goal, so you reserve extra time to spend on harder questions. When you budget extra time for the harder questions, you no longer have any reason to stress when those questions take longer to answer.

Don't let this time expectation distract you from working through the test at a calm, steady pace, but keep it in mind so you don't spend too much time on any one question. Recognize that taking extra time on one question you don't understand may keep you from answering two that you do understand later in the test. If your time limit for a question is up and you're still not sure of the answer, mark it and move on, and come back to it later if the time and the test format allow. If the testing format doesn't allow you to return to earlier questions, just make an educated guess; then put it out of your mind and move on.

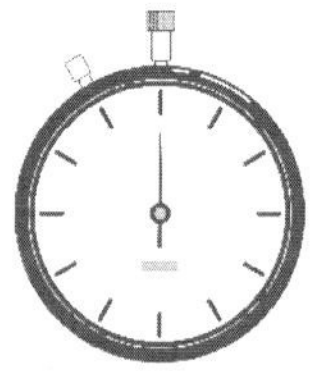

On the easier questions, be careful not to rush. It may seem wise to hurry through them so you have more time for the challenging ones, but it's not worth missing one if you know the concept and just didn't take the time to read the question fully. Work efficiently but make sure you understand the question and have looked at all of the answer choices, since more than one may seem right at first.

Even if you're paying attention to the time, you may find yourself a little behind at some point. You should speed up to get back on track, but do so wisely. Don't panic; just take a few seconds less on each question until you're caught up. Don't guess without thinking, but do look through the answer choices and eliminate any you know are wrong. If you can get down to two choices, it is often worthwhile to guess from those. Once you've chosen an answer, move on and don't dwell on any that you skipped or had to hurry through. If a question was taking too long, chances are it was one of the harder ones, so you weren't as likely to get it right anyway.

On the other hand, if you find yourself getting ahead of schedule, it may be beneficial to slow down a little. The more quickly you work, the more likely you are to make a careless mistake that will affect your score. You've budgeted time for each question, so don't be afraid to spend that time. Practice an efficient but careful pace to get the most out of the time you have.

Secret Key #5 – Have a Plan for Guessing

When you're taking the test, you may find yourself stuck on a question. Some of the answer choices seem better than others, but you don't see the one answer choice that is obviously correct. What do you do?

The scenario described above is very common, yet most test takers have not effectively prepared for it. Developing and practicing a plan for guessing may be one of the single most effective uses of your time as you get ready for the exam.

In developing your plan for guessing, there are three questions to address:

- When should you start the guessing process?
- How should you narrow down the choices?
- Which answer should you choose?

When to Start the Guessing Process

Unless your plan for guessing is to select C every time (which, despite its merits, is not what we recommend), you need to leave yourself enough time to apply your answer elimination strategies. Since you have a limited amount of time for each question, that means that if you're going to give yourself the best shot at guessing correctly, you have to decide quickly whether or not you will guess.

Of course, the best-case scenario is that you don't have to guess at all, so first, see if you can answer the question based on your knowledge of the subject and basic reasoning skills. Focus on the key words in the question and try to jog your memory of related topics. Give yourself a chance to bring the knowledge to mind, but once you realize that you don't have (or you can't access) the knowledge you need to answer the question, it's time to start the guessing process.

It's almost always better to start the guessing process too early than too late. It only takes a few seconds to remember something and answer the question from knowledge. Carefully eliminating wrong answer choices takes longer. Plus, going through the process of eliminating answer choices can actually help jog your memory.

Summary: Start the guessing process as soon as you decide that you can't answer the question based on your knowledge.

How to Narrow Down the Choices

The next chapter in this book (**Test-Taking Strategies**) includes a wide range of strategies for how to approach questions and how to look for answer choices to eliminate. You will definitely want to read those carefully, practice them, and figure out which ones work best for you. Here though, we're going to address a mindset rather than a particular strategy.

Your odds of guessing an answer correctly depend on how many options you are choosing from.

Number of options left	5	4	3	2	1
Odds of guessing correctly	20%	25%	33%	50%	100%

You can see from this chart just how valuable it is to be able to eliminate incorrect answers and make an educated guess, but there are two things that many test takers do that cause them to miss out on the benefits of guessing:

- Accidentally eliminating the correct answer
- Selecting an answer based on an impression

We'll look at the first one here, and the second one in the next section.

To avoid accidentally eliminating the correct answer, we recommend a thought exercise called **the $5 challenge**. In this challenge, you only eliminate an answer choice from contention if you are willing to bet $5 on it being wrong. Why $5? Five dollars is a small but not insignificant amount of money. It's an amount you could afford to lose but wouldn't want to throw away. And while losing $5 once might not hurt too much, doing it twenty times will set you back $100. In the same way, each small decision you make—eliminating a choice here, guessing on a question there—won't by itself impact your score very much, but when you put them all together, they can make a big difference. By holding each answer choice elimination decision to a higher standard, you can reduce the risk of accidentally eliminating the correct answer.

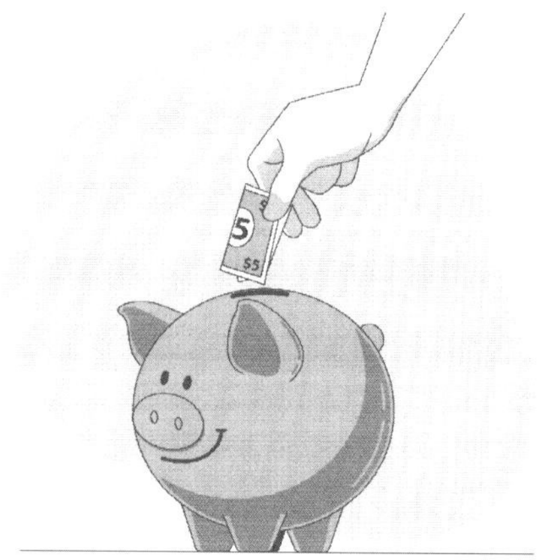

The $5 challenge can also be applied in a positive sense: If you are willing to bet $5 that an answer choice *is* correct, go ahead and mark it as correct.

Summary: Only eliminate an answer choice if you are willing to bet $5 that it is wrong.

Which Answer to Choose

You're taking the test. You've run into a hard question and decided you'll have to guess. You've eliminated all the answer choices you're willing to bet $5 on. Now you have to pick an answer. Why do we even need to talk about this? Why can't you just pick whichever one you feel like when the time comes?

The answer to these questions is that if you don't come into the test with a plan, you'll rely on your impression to select an answer choice, and if you do that, you risk falling into a trap. The test writers know that everyone who takes their test will be guessing on some of the questions, so they intentionally write wrong answer choices to seem plausible. You still have to pick an answer though, and if the wrong answer choices are designed to look right, how can you ever be sure that you're not falling for their trap? The best solution we've found to this dilemma is to take the decision out of your hands entirely. Here is the process we recommend:

Once you've eliminated any choices that you are confident (willing to bet $5) are wrong, select the first remaining choice as your answer.

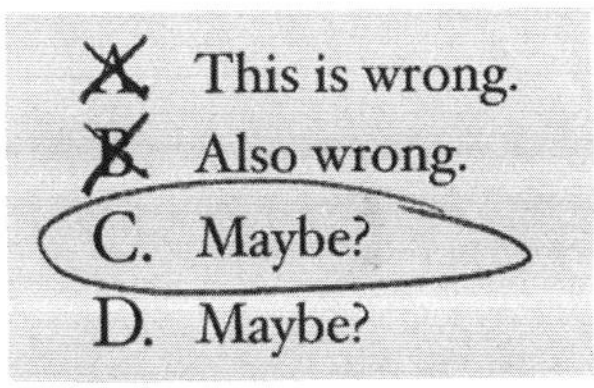

Whether you choose to select the first remaining choice, the second, or the last, the important thing is that you use some preselected standard. Using this approach guarantees that you will not be enticed into selecting an answer choice that looks right, because you are not basing your decision on how the answer choices look.

This is not meant to make you question your knowledge. Instead, it is to help you recognize the difference between your knowledge and your impressions. There's a huge difference between thinking an answer is right because of what you know, and thinking an answer is right because it looks or sounds like it should be right.

Summary: To ensure that your selection is appropriately random, make a predetermined selection from among all answer choices you have not eliminated.

Test-Taking Strategies

This section contains a list of test-taking strategies that you may find helpful as you work through the test. By taking what you know and applying logical thought, you can maximize your chances of answering any question correctly!

It is very important to realize that every question is different and every person is different: no single strategy will work on every question, and no single strategy will work for every person. That's why we've included all of them here, so you can try them out and determine which ones work best for different types of questions and which ones work best for you.

Question Strategies

☑ Read Carefully

Read the question and the answer choices carefully. Don't miss the question because you misread the terms. You have plenty of time to read each question thoroughly and make sure you understand what is being asked. Yet a happy medium must be attained, so don't waste too much time. You must read carefully and efficiently.

☑ Contextual Clues

Look for contextual clues. If the question includes a word you are not familiar with, look at the immediate context for some indication of what the word might mean. Contextual clues can often give you all the information you need to decipher the meaning of an unfamiliar word. Even if you can't determine the meaning, you may be able to narrow down the possibilities enough to make a solid guess at the answer to the question.

☑ Prefixes

If you're having trouble with a word in the question or answer choices, try dissecting it. Take advantage of every clue that the word might include. Prefixes can be a huge help. Usually, they allow you to determine a basic meaning. *Pre-* means before, *post-* means after, *pro-* is positive, *de-* is negative. From prefixes, you can get an idea of the general meaning of the word and try to put it into context.

☑ Hedge Words

Watch out for critical hedge words, such as *likely, may, can, often, almost, mostly, usually, generally, rarely*, and *sometimes*. Question writers insert these hedge phrases to cover every possibility. Often an answer choice will be wrong simply because it leaves no room for exception. Be on guard for answer choices that have definitive words such as *exactly* and *always*.

☑ Switchback Words

Stay alert for *switchbacks*. These are the words and phrases frequently used to alert you to shifts in thought. The most common switchback words are *but, although*, and *however*. Others include *nevertheless, on the other hand, even though, while, in spite of, despite*, and *regardless of*. Switchback words are important to catch because they can change the direction of the question or an answer choice.

FACE VALUE

When in doubt, use common sense. Accept the situation in the problem at face value. Don't read too much into it. These problems will not require you to make wild assumptions. If you have to go beyond creativity and warp time or space in order to have an answer choice fit the question, then you should move on and consider the other answer choices. These are normal problems rooted in reality. The applicable relationship or explanation may not be readily apparent, but it is there for you to figure out. Use your common sense to interpret anything that isn't clear.

Answer Choice Strategies

ANSWER SELECTION

The most thorough way to pick an answer choice is to identify and eliminate wrong answers until only one is left, then confirm it is the correct answer. Sometimes an answer choice may immediately seem right, but be careful. The test writers will usually put more than one reasonable answer choice on each question, so take a second to read all of them and make sure that the other choices are not equally obvious. As long as you have time left, it is better to read every answer choice than to pick the first one that looks right without checking the others.

ANSWER CHOICE FAMILIES

An answer choice family consists of two (in rare cases, three) answer choices that are very similar in construction and cannot all be true at the same time. If you see two answer choices that are direct opposites or parallels, one of them is usually the correct answer. For instance, if one answer choice says that quantity *x* increases and another either says that quantity *x* decreases (opposite) or says that quantity *y* increases (parallel), then those answer choices would fall into the same family. An answer choice that doesn't match the construction of the answer choice family is more likely to be incorrect. Most questions will not have answer choice families, but when they do appear, you should be prepared to recognize them.

ELIMINATE ANSWERS

Eliminate answer choices as soon as you realize they are wrong, but make sure you consider all possibilities. If you are eliminating answer choices and realize that the last one you are left with is also wrong, don't panic. Start over and consider each choice again. There may be something you missed the first time that you will realize on the second pass.

AVOID FACT TRAPS

Don't be distracted by an answer choice that is factually true but doesn't answer the question. You are looking for the choice that answers the question. Stay focused on what the question is asking for so you don't accidentally pick an answer that is true but incorrect. Always go back to the question and make sure the answer choice you've selected actually answers the question and is not merely a true statement.

EXTREME STATEMENTS

In general, you should avoid answers that put forth extreme actions as standard practice or proclaim controversial ideas as established fact. An answer choice that states the "process should be used in certain situations, if..." is much more likely to be correct than one that states the "process should be discontinued completely." The first is a calm rational statement and doesn't even make a definitive, uncompromising stance, using a hedge word *if* to provide wiggle room, whereas the second choice is far more extreme.

⊘ BENCHMARK

As you read through the answer choices and you come across one that seems to answer the question well, mentally select that answer choice. This is not your final answer, but it's the one that will help you evaluate the other answer choices. The one that you selected is your benchmark or standard for judging each of the other answer choices. Every other answer choice must be compared to your benchmark. That choice is correct until proven otherwise by another answer choice beating it. If you find a better answer, then that one becomes your new benchmark. Once you've decided that no other choice answers the question as well as your benchmark, you have your final answer.

⊘ PREDICT THE ANSWER

Before you even start looking at the answer choices, it is often best to try to predict the answer. When you come up with the answer on your own, it is easier to avoid distractions and traps because you will know exactly what to look for. The right answer choice is unlikely to be word-for-word what you came up with, but it should be a close match. Even if you are confident that you have the right answer, you should still take the time to read each option before moving on.

General Strategies

⊘ TOUGH QUESTIONS

If you are stumped on a problem or it appears too hard or too difficult, don't waste time. Move on! Remember though, if you can quickly check for obviously incorrect answer choices, your chances of guessing correctly are greatly improved. Before you completely give up, at least try to knock out a couple of possible answers. Eliminate what you can and then guess at the remaining answer choices before moving on.

⊘ CHECK YOUR WORK

Since you will probably not know every term listed and the answer to every question, it is important that you get credit for the ones that you do know. Don't miss any questions through careless mistakes. If at all possible, try to take a second to look back over your answer selection and make sure you've selected the correct answer choice and haven't made a costly careless mistake (such as marking an answer choice that you didn't mean to mark). This quick double check should more than pay for itself in caught mistakes for the time it costs.

⊘ PACE YOURSELF

It's easy to be overwhelmed when you're looking at a page full of questions; your mind is confused and full of random thoughts, and the clock is ticking down faster than you would like. Calm down and maintain the pace that you have set for yourself. Especially as you get down to the last few minutes of the test, don't let the small numbers on the clock make you panic. As long as you are on track by monitoring your pace, you are guaranteed to have time for each question.

⊘ DON'T RUSH

It is very easy to make errors when you are in a hurry. Maintaining a fast pace in answering questions is pointless if it makes you miss questions that you would have gotten right otherwise. Test writers like to include distracting information and wrong answers that seem right. Taking a little extra time to avoid careless mistakes can make all the difference in your test score. Find a pace that allows you to be confident in the answers that you select.

✓ Keep Moving

Panicking will not help you pass the test, so do your best to stay calm and keep moving. Taking deep breaths and going through the answer elimination steps you practiced can help to break through a stress barrier and keep your pace.

Final Notes

The combination of a solid foundation of content knowledge and the confidence that comes from practicing your plan for applying that knowledge is the key to maximizing your performance on test day. As your foundation of content knowledge is built up and strengthened, you'll find that the strategies included in this chapter become more and more effective in helping you quickly sift through the distractions and traps of the test to isolate the correct answer.

Now that you're preparing to move forward into the test content chapters of this book, be sure to keep your goal in mind. As you read, think about how you will be able to apply this information on the test. If you've already seen sample questions for the test and you have an idea of the question format and style, try to come up with questions of your own that you can answer based on what you're reading. This will give you valuable practice applying your knowledge in the same ways you can expect to on test day.

Good luck and good studying!

Reading Prose and Poetry

Prose

In China, New Year's Day is a day for great celebrations. People have big parades, and some of them dress up like a monster called Nian. Almost every family glues red paper to their front doors, keeps the lights on in every room of the house until after midnight, and lights fireworks. This Chinese folk tale explains why they do these things.

How Nian Was Defeated

Once upon a time, near the village of Taohun (Peach Blossom), there lived a huge beast at the bottom of the sea. His name was Nian, and once a year, on New Year's Day, he would come forth out of the sea for one day. After spending all year at the bottom of the ocean, Nian was very hungry. He would eat just about everything he could see. He ate the crops, and he ate the cows, pigs and horses. He ate pets, too. He still wasn't satisfied, though, so he would even eat human beings. Nian especially loved to eat children. If he couldn't find anything to eat, he would get so angry he would destroy everything in his path.

Chinese New Year Lion Dance Costume

The people who lived in Taohun were very afraid of Nian. So on New Year's Eve, the day before Nian's arrival, they would flee the village so he wouldn't eat them. The entire village would head to the top of the faraway mountains so that Nian couldn't find them. If they had animals, they would try to take them with them. Every year, though, Nian managed to catch and eat some of the slowest villagers. All year long the villagers lived in dread, knowing that Nian would come out of the ocean on New Year's Day. Even if they managed to avoid being eaten, when they came back to the village they would have to rebuild everything Nian had destroyed.

One year an old beggar wandered into the village on New Year's Eve. He went from house to house asking for a bite to eat, but everyone ignored him. They were terrified of the monster, and they were hurrying as fast as they could to get ready to flee the village. Finally an old lady who lived right by the ocean felt sorry for the beggar. She gave him a bite to eat, but then warned him to flee. "Don't you know what day it is tomorrow? Get to the mountains before Nian eats you!"

But the old beggar wasn't scared. Instead, he smiled mysteriously. When the woman asked him how he could smile at a time like this, he simply replied, "Ma'am, if you will shelter me in your house for one evening, I will see to it that Nian never terrorizes the village again." The old woman looked at him like he was crazy. Before long it would be dark, and there wasn't much time to spare. "Look, you can't stay in my house. Nian will be coming soon, so you must flee for your life!" But the old man didn't say anything; he just kept smiling mysteriously. Finally the woman decided that there was no more time to argue with him, and she shook her head sadly as she walked out of the house and headed for the mountains. There was nothing more she could do. If the old beggar was foolish enough to stay in her house, he would be sorry.

Soon enough, everyone in the village was gone, except for the old beggar in the house. They had all fled to the mountains for safety. At one second past midnight, Nian rose from the bottom of the ocean, just as he did every year. The first house he came to was the old lady's, and he prepared to knock it down in search of something to eat. But just as he started to run toward the door, he noticed something was different this year. There was red paper glued to the door. He was scared of the color red. The house was lit up in every room, and that frightened him even more. Then fireworks started going off, which terrified him. Quivering like a leaf, Nian tucked his tail between his legs and ran back into the ocean.

The next day all the people of the village came home. They were shocked to discover that there was no damage to the village at all. They were puzzled and happy at the same time, and they all began to ask each other why Nian hadn't destroyed the village this year. The old lady told them about the strange beggar, and the promise he had made to her. Filled with curiosity and excitement, everyone ran over to the old lady's house. They saw the red paper on the door, all the candles burning in the house, and the used fireworks in the yard. They wondered what it could mean. Then the old beggar came out of the house and explained to them that Nian was afraid of lights, the color red, and loud noises. After that, every year on New Year's Eve, the people of Peach Blossom glued red paper to their doors, lit candles in every room, and set off fireworks to keep Nian away, and he never troubled them again.

QUESTIONS

1. In paragraph 1, which word means the same thing as *sea*?

____

____

2. In paragraph 5, what does *quivering* mean?

____

____

3. In paragraph 2, what does *dread* mean?

____

____

4. What is the central lesson of this story?

____

____

5. Which of these books does this story have the most in common with?

a. *The Story of George Washington*
b. *The History of the United States*
c. *The Legend of Paul Bunyan*
d. *How to Play Baseball*

Poetry

A Jelly-Fish

By: Marianne Moore

Visible, invisible,
A fluctuating charm,
An amber-colored amethyst
Inhabits it; your arm
Approaches, and
It opens and
It closes;
You have meant
To catch it,
And it shrivels;
You abandon
Your intent—
It opens, and it
Closes and you
Reach for it—
The blue
Surrounding it
Grows cloudy, and
It floats away
From you.

There Was A Small Boy Of Quebec

By: Rudyard Kipling

THERE was a small boy of Quebec,
Who was buried in snow to his neck;
When they said. "Are you friz?"
He replied, "Yes, I is—
But we don't call this cold in Quebec."

Old Pond

By: Matsuo Basho

The old pond—
The frog jumps in:
The sound of water

Bed in Summer

By: Robert Louis Stevenson

In winter I get up at night
And dress by yellow candle-light.
In summer, quite the other way,
I have to go to bed by day.

I have to go to bed and see
The birds still hopping on the tree,
Or hear the grown-up people's feet
Still going past me in the street.

And does it not seem hard to you,
When all the sky is clear and blue,
And I should like so much to play,
To have to go to bed by day?

Questions

1. What type of poem is *A Jelly-Fish*?

a. Free verse
b. Rhymed verse
c. Haiku
d. Limerick

2. What type of poem is *There Was A Small Boy Of Quebec?*

a. Free verse
b. Rhymed verse
c. Haiku
d. Limerick

3. What type of poem is *Old Pond*?

a. Free verse
b. Rhymed verse
c. Haiku
d. Limerick

4. What type of poem is *Bed in Summer*?

a. Free verse
b. Rhymed verse
c. Haiku
d. Limerick

5. What do all four poems have in common?

a. Form and structure
b. Perspective
c. Simplicity
d. Culture

Reading Informational Texts

Our Neighbor Mercury

1 Earth is a planet with many neighbors. Besides Earth, there are seven other full sized planets in the solar system, and the one that is the closest to the sun is named Mercury. Earth is about two and a half times the size of Mercury. The surface of Mercury is very rough, like our moon. There are lots of craters, and it is completely barren, with nothing but soil as far as the eye can see. Do you know how Mercury got its name? The name comes from ancient Rome, some 24 centuries ago. The Romans believed in many different gods, and the messenger of the gods was called Mercury. He was able to move extremely fast. Because this planet moves around the sun faster than any other planets, it was given the name Mercury.

2 Sometimes Mercury is closer to our planet than at other times, but it is always a long way away. The closest it ever gets to us is about 40 million miles. It is much closer to the sun than Earth is, so it doesn't take it nearly as long to revolve around the sun. In fact, it only takes 88 days for Mercury to orbit the sun. So, here on earth a year is 365 days long, but on Mercury a year is only 88 days long. So, if you're 10 years old, if you lived on Mercury you would be almost 42 years old!

3 If that's not strange enough, consider this. Earth orbits around the sun, and it also rotates, like a spinning top. One full rotation is 24 hours, or one day. Well, Mercury also rotates, but much more slowly. A day on Mercury is 58 Earth days. Since a year on Mercury is only 88 Earth days, that means there are only one and a half "days" in a Mercury year. That would be like the sun coming up on Earth and then it would be sunny 24 hours a day for four months, and then it would be dark for four months straight, and then sunny again for four months. That would be very hard to get used to, so living on Mercury with a day that is actually 58 Earth days long would be quite a change.

4 Of course, there's no chance that anyone will ever actually live on Mercury. It's impossible, because of the temperatures on the planet. Temperatures can range from 300 degrees below zero to around 800 degrees. 800 degrees is hot enough to melt some metals. We would broil to death almost instantly on Mercury. When it got dark, we would freeze to death. Some people believe that one of these days an astronaut will walk on Mars, but that will never happen on Mercury!

Questions

1. Using the information you learned in this article, find Mercury on this map and circle it. (The big item on the left is the Sun, and Earth is the third planet away from the sun.)

2. What is the main purpose of this story?

a. to explain how long a year is
b. to discuss the entire solar system
c. to give facts about the sun
d. to give facts about the planet Mercury

3. What word in paragraph 1 means huge holes?

____

____

4. Why do you think it gets so much hotter on Mercury than on Earth? Use evidence from the text to support your answer.

____

____

MONTANA: BIG SKY COUNTRY

1 Most people know that Alaska is the biggest state. Many people know that Texas is 2nd, and California is 3rd. Lots of people know the top three, but do you know which state is 4th when it comes to size? It's Montana. (It's also the biggest state that doesn't border a large body of water.)

Glacier National Park, Montana

2 This massive state (over 147,000 square miles) is located in the northwest area of the US. It became the 41st state when it was admitted to the Union on November 8, 1889. Montana is bordered by four states – North Dakota, South Dakota, Wyoming, and Idaho. It is also bordered by another country, Canada.

3 Many people believe that Montana is one of the most scenic states. It certainly does have a lot of natural beauty. Its name means "mountain" in Spanish, and there are certainly lots of mountains there. Most mountains are on the western side of the state; the rest of the state is basically flat. Montana also contains many national and state parks. Part of Yellowstone National Park, one of the most famous natural attractions in the world, is in Montana. The state is also full of wildlife not found in most states, such as bighorn sheep, mountain lions, mountain goats, elk, bobcats, lynx, bison, black bears, and grizzly bears, to name just a few.

4 Montana has several nicknames. One of them is "Big Sky Country", and another is "The Treasure State." The latter nickname refers to the fact that mining used to be a big industry in Montana, and that many people came to the area back in the 1800s searching for gold. These days, farming is the most common business in the state. Farmers in Montana raise lots of wheat, hay, barley and other

crops. There are over two and a half million head of cattle in the state, and hundreds of thousands of sheep.

Bighorn Sheep in Montana

5 One of the most famous battles in American history took place in Montana. It's officially known as Battle of the Little Bighorn, but many people call it Custer's Last Stand. Many Native Americans call it the Battle of the Greasy Grass. It took place in 1876, when Montana was still part of a territory, and not a state yet. It was a battle between the US Army and two Native American tribes, the Lakota and the Cheyenne. The battle has become legendary because the Native Americans outnumbered the Army, and defeated them badly. General George Custer and almost 300 soldiers died on the battlefield. The battlefield is now a national monument. So Montana is not only full of beauty and natural resources, but it's also rich in history.

Questions

1. If you had to choose another title for this article, which of these would be best?

a. Let's Explore Montana
b. Montana's Biggest Mountain
c. The Montana Gold Rush
d. Why People Don't Like Montana

2. What is the author's purpose of this piece?

a. To entertain
b. To inform
c. To persuade
d. None of the above

3. What is the best summary for this passage?

a. Montana is the fifth largest state, and it is home to scenic beauty, wildlife, historical milestones, farming, and mining.
b. Montana is the fourth largest state, and it is home to mountains, deserts, valleys, historical milestones, and tourism.
c. Montana is the fifth largest state, and it is home to mountains, deserts, valleys, historical milestones, and tourism.
d. Montana is the fourth largest state, and it is home to scenic beauty, wildlife, historical milestones, farming, and mining.

4. What does the word "massive" mean in paragraph two?

a. Very heavy
b. Very small or tiny
c. Very light
d. Very large or enormous

LINDA RICHARDS, MEDICAL PIONEER

1 All Americans should be thankful for Linda Richards. Who was she? Well, let me explain. Just about everyone has been to the doctor, and many of us have had to spend some time in a hospital. Most of us don't like going to the doctor's office, and nobody looks forward to going to the hospital. It's no fun to be sick, get shots, have tests, or be confined to a bed.

Linda Richards

2 However, there are people whose job it is to take care of us while we're being treated by doctors. They are called nurses, and they have helped hundreds of millions of Americans feel better and get well faster over the years. All of us should be grateful for nurses, because nearly all of us have been helped by a nurse at one time or another, and we all have several family members who have been brought back to health thanks to the efforts of nurses. Well, Linda Richards is one of the "Founding Mothers" of modern nursing.

3 Linda Richards was born in West Potsdam, New York, in 1841. Her father was a preacher, and he wanted Linda to become a missionary after she grew up. However, her father died when she was only four years old. Then her mother became very sick, and Linda spent years taking care of her mother until she died when Linda was fourteen. A lot of people would feel sorry for themselves if both their parents died when they were young, and they might never get over it. Linda Richards was different, though. She had enjoyed taking care of her mother, and she decided that she was going to become a nurse, and not a missionary.

4 Linda Richards wasn't the first nurse in the world by any stretch of the imagination. Nurses have been around for centuries, but until recently, nursing was a lot different than it is today. Back in the old days, most nurses weren't very educated. Some of them couldn't read or write, and they knew little about medicine or health. They mostly did things to make patients feel more comfortable, such as give them a drink of water, help them go to the bathroom, or wipe their foreheads with a wet rag. These tasks are very important, but there is a lot more a nurse needs to know and do to help people get well. Linda Richards understood that, and she helped change nursing into the modern profession it is today.

5 After helping a local doctor for a while, she took a nursing job at a hospital in Boston, but it was an awful experience. There was no training, and nurses were expected to work from 6 in the morning to 9:30 at night. They also had to sleep at the hospital, near their patients, and would have to get up

every time a patient called them. This was very hard on nurses, and many of them quit. Linda was one of them, and she soon became a student in the first class ever held at America's very first nursing school. After she graduated, she became a supervisor at Bellevue Hospital in New York City. While she worked there, she invented a way of keeping records for each patient. It might sound hard to believe, but until Linda Richards came along, most hospitals didn't keep very good track of their patients and their health. She changed all that, and before long all hospitals in America were keeping patient records.

6 She didn't stop there. Linda Richards kept getting more education for herself. She even went to England to study with Florence Nightingale, the most famous nurse in history. After she returned to America, she began starting nursing schools across the country in order to train people in the modern methods of nursing. Pretty soon, nurses who had an education in health and medicine were helping patients all over America. Linda Richards did more than anyone else has ever done to improve nursing in America, and thanks to her, millions of people have lived longer and better lives.

Florence Nightingale

QUESTIONS

1. Which of these helped Linda Richards decide to become a nurse?

a. coming down with the flu
b. seeing a vision from God
c. taking care of her sick mother
d. her pet cat dying

2. Which of these is NOT something Linda Richards did?

a. created a system of keeping records for hospital patients
b. discovered a new medicine
c. attended the first nursing school in America
d. founded several nursing schools

3. Put the following events from Linda Richards' life in order, writing 1, 2, 3, or 4 beside each one

______ She went to England to study with Florence Nightingale
______ She took care of her dying mother
______ She invented a record keeping system
______ She took a job at Bellevue Hospital

Reading Across Genres & Vocabulary

The Big Picture

Chapter 1: Mom's Big Idea

1 "This has got to stop!"

2 Janey could tell that her mom was exasperated. She watched from the hallway as her mother stared out the living room window as one car after another whizzed by their house.

3 "What's wrong, Mom?" Janey asked.

4 "These cars and trucks flying down the road, that's what. It's dangerous, and if something isn't done about it someone is going to get run over one of these days. It's just a matter of time. The city needs to lower the speed limit to 35 miles per hour. A few years ago, when there were very few houses out here, a speed limit of 55 miles per hour was fine, but not anymore. We've got to do something about this."

5 "Why don't you call City Hall and ask them to change the speed limit?"

6 "I already have, Janey. I've called several times, I've emailed, and I've even gone down there in person, but I can't get anyone to do anything about the problem. It's like nobody down there cares."

7 Janey was curious. "What are you going to do, Mom?"

8 "I'm not sure yet. I'll have to ponder it for a while."

9 Just then Janey's father pulled into the driveway. "Janey, Dad's home. Finish setting the table."

10 "Okay, Mom."

11 In a few minutes the family was gathered around the table for dinner. Janey listened as her mother and father discussed the problem of the speeding cars at length. As they were clearing the table, Janey asked her mom if she had come up with any ideas yet. Her mom said she had a great idea.

12 "What is it, Mom? Are you going to write a letter to the newspaper? Are you going to protest in front of City Hall?"

13 Then Janey's dad joined in. "Are you're going to go door to door collecting signatures for a petition? What's your idea, dear? Don't keep us in the dark."

14 "Well," Janey's mom replied, "those are all excellent ideas, and I might try some of them later, if I need to. But I have another idea – I'm going to create a website about the speeding problem."

15 "Wow! A website! Mom, that's a great idea!" Janey exclaimed.

16 "Thanks, honey", said Janey's mom, laughing. "I just hope the community will be as excited about the website as you are!"

Questions

1. In paragraph 4, Janey's mom uses some figurative language. In the blank space below, write the figurative phrase, and then explain what it actually means.

____

____

2. In paragraph 2, what does *exasperated* mean?

a. very bored
b. very happy
c. very angry
d. very hungry

3. In paragraph 8, what does *ponder* mean?

a. write a letter about
b. think about
c. talk about
d. look up in a dictionary

4. In paragraph 13, Janey's dad uses figurative language. In the blank space below, write the figurative phrase, and then explain what it actually means.

____

____

5. What is the main idea of this passage?

a. speeding vehicles are dangerous
b. nobody at City Hall cares about speeding vehicles
c. discussing things at dinner is a good way to solve problems
d. Janey's mom decides to make a website about the speeding vehicle problem

Chapter 2: Mom Makes a List

1 Janey came in from riding her bike to get a drink of water and rest for a few minutes. She filled her glass and then sat down at the dining room table with her mom, who was writing in a notebook. "What are you writing about, Mom?" Janey inquired.

2 "I'm just making a few notes, dear. It's sort of a checklist of everything I need to do to get my new website up and running."

3 "Can I see your list?"

4 "Sure, Janey." Her mom smiled and handed her the notebook. "Let me know what you think."

5 Janey looked at her mom's list:

- Think of a website name.
- Think of a domain name.
- Buy the domain.
- Compare hosting plans.
- Buy hosting.
- Install blog software.
- Install forum software.
- Choose graphics, layout and design.

6 "Gosh, Mom! Hosting, graphics, blog, domain...I don't know what a lot of these words even mean."

7 Her mom laughed. "Don't worry about that stuff, dear. It's a lot of technical jargon. Until I started looking into how to create a website, I didn't know what some of those words meant, either."

8 "Boy oh boy, there's a lot more to making a website than I thought there was. It sounds really complicated."

9 "It does at first, doesn't it?" her mom replied. "Actually, though, it's really not very complicated at all. You just have to do a little research to make sure you've got all your ducks in a row."

10 "Well, Mom, I'm still glad you're the one who's doing it, and not me. I couldn't figure that stuff out in a million years."

11 Her mom laughed again. "A million? Ha! In just a few years you'll know so much about this stuff you'll be able to run circles around me!"

12 "You may be right, Mom. But right now I've got more important things to do, like riding my bike."

13 Janey and her mom both laughed as she grabbed her helmet and headed out the door.

QUESTIONS

1. In paragraph 1, what does *inquired* mean?

a. whispered
b. yelled
c. asked
d. told

2. In paragraph 7, what does *jargon* mean?

a. special words or phrases about a particular topic
b. baby talk
c. nonsense
d. expensive tools

3. In paragraph 9, Janey's mom uses some figurative language. In the blank space below, write the figurative phrase, and then explain what it actually means.

____

____

4. Divide the following words into syllables, like this: baseball <u>base | ball</u>

a. million ____________
b. domain____________
c. technical ____________
d. hosting____________

5. In paragraph 8, what does *complicated* mean?

a. easy to understand
b. difficult to understand
c. lots of fun
d. very boring

Chapter 3: Mom Launches Her Website

1 "Please pass the syrup, Dad," Janey said as she buttered her pancakes. She loved Saturday mornings. On Saturdays everybody slept in, and then the family always had pancakes for a late breakfast. "No alarm clock and pancakes make a great combination," thought Janey. There was something that was a little bit different this Saturday morning, though. At first, Janey couldn't quite put her finger on it. Then she suddenly realized what was different.

2 "*Mom!* That's got to be the fifth time you've yawned since we started breakfast. That's not like you at all. I'm the one who's usually yawning at the breakfast table."

3 Her mom started to reply, but then yawned again.

4 "Now, now, Janey, there's no need to reprimand your mother," Janey's dad said with a wink. "Don't worry; she's not turning into a night owl. She has a valid excuse for being tired. She was up until almost three in the morning putting the finishing touches on her website."

5 "Really, Mom? It's finally done and ready to go?"

6 "It sure is, Janey," her mom replied. "In fact, it's not just ready to go. It's actually 'on the air' right now. I published my first article right before I went to bed."

7 "Alright, Mom! Way to go!"

8 "Thanks, Janey, but this is only the beginning. There's still a lot of work to do. Let's not forget that the only reason I started this website is to get the speed limit on our street lowered to 35 miles an hour. The website is only a tool to help me accomplish that."

9 "I know, Mom, but it's still exciting, and I'm proud of you. I bet I'm the only one in my class whose mom has a website."

10 "Well, how would you like to help me with my website *and* be the star of your very own video on the internet?"

11 "That would be awesome, Mom!"

12 "I thought you might be interested," said Janey's mom, as she winked at Janey's dad. "Okay, then, we have a deal. We'll make the video next Friday after you get home from school. Of course, that's only if the weather is good, because we'll be making the video outside."

13 Janey was a bit disappointed. "Friday? Why can't we do it today, or Monday?"

14 "Well, we can't do it today because there's not as much traffic on Saturdays. I want the video to show people just how bad the problem is. And we can't do it on Monday, because you'll need time to memorize your script."

15 "I'm going to have a script? Really?"

16 "Yes, and I'm going to start writing it today, so you'll have all week to memorize it."

17 "Well, Mom and Dad, please excuse me from the breakfast table. If I'm going to be a movie star, I'd better start acting like one. If you need me, I'll be in my dressing room."

Questions

1. In paragraph 1, what does this sentence mean: "At first, Janey couldn't quite put her finger on it."

____

____

2. In paragraph 4, what does *reprimand* mean?

a. ignore
b. slap on the face
c. stare at
d. severely scold

3. Janey's dad is using figurative language when he tells Janey that her mom is not turning into a "night owl." What does "night owl" mean in that sentence?

____

____

4. In paragraph 4, what does *valid* mean?

a. fake
b. not true
c. good
d. sleepy

5. Which word below does NOT have the same meaning as *accomplish* in paragraph 8?

a. stop
b. do
c. achieve
d. fulfill

Chapter 4: Lights! Camera! Janey!

1 Today was the big day - Janey was going be in a video for her mom's website. She had completely memorized her script by Tuesday, and she made it a point to rehearse her lines every night after school. Now Friday was finally here. Janey couldn't wait to get home and make the video. Normally she loved going to school, but today it seemed to drag on forever. Finally, the last bell of the day rang, and before she knew it the school bus was stopping in front of her house and dropping her off.

2 "Mom! I'm home!" Janey exclaimed as she opened the door and walked in. "Are we ready to start the video?"

3 Janey's mom was sitting at the kitchen table. "I'm in here, dear. Are you sure you're ready?"

4 "I sure am, Mom. I know every word of the script by heart."

5 "Okay, then. Let's make a video!"

6 They went outside to the front yard. Janey stood quietly while her mom looked for the best place for her to stand. "Alright, this looks like a great spot. If you stand here the viewers will be able to see you, and all the traffic."

7 Janey moved to the spot her mother had picked out. "Okay, Mom, I'm ready when you are."

8 "Okay, Janey. Stand there for a moment while I adjust the settings on the camera, and try not to fidget."

9 Janey stood as still as possible while her mom tried to get the distance and focus just right. Finally, her mom was satisfied, and it was time to get started.

10 "When you see the red light on the camera come on, that will be your signal to start talking. You'll need to speak up, but don't yell. We've got plenty of time, so if you make a mistake, it's no big deal. We'll just start over. Now, look right into the camera, and when you see the red light, start talking."

11 Janey was nervous as she took a deep breath, and waited for the red light. There it was! She gave the camera a big smile, and started talking.

12 "Hi! My name is Janey Peterson, and I'm making this video to alert the local community to a hazardous situation. I'm standing in the front yard of my house, which is located on Old Mill Road. My family and I love living here, except for one thing. The speed limit is too high, and it's making things dangerous. We moved here five years ago and there were hardly any other houses out here, and there was very little traffic. Having a 55 mile per hour speed limit wasn't a problem then. Things have changed, however. Since then, lots of families have built houses on Old Mill Road, and several factories have been built a few miles from here. Hundreds of people work in these factories, and a lot of them use our road for a shortcut. So do many other people. As you can see, one car after another is speeding down the road right behind me. This goes on constantly, and it's very dangerous. If something isn't done, it's only a matter of time before someone is injured. My mom has called, emailed and visited City Hall to try to get the speed limit lowered, but nothing has been done. So we're asking for your help. Please contact the folks at City Hall and ask them to lower the speed limit on Old Mill Road to 35 miles per hour before someone gets hurt. Thank you."

13 "That was great, Janey!"

14 "Was it really that good, Mom?" Janey asked

15 "It sure was!"

16 "Do you want me to do it again? I don't mind."

17 "No, Janey, that won't be necessary. You did a great job. Now let's go put this video on my website."

QUESTIONS

1. In paragraph 1, what does *rehearse* mean?

a. write down
b. say into a recorder
c. practice
d. forget

2. In paragraph 8, Janey's mom asks her to try not to *fidget*. What word below has the same meaning as *fidget*?

a. giggle
b. squirm
c. whisper
d. blink

3. Which of these words would NOT be a good replacement for *satisfied* in paragraph 9?

a. happy
b. content
c. pleased
d. upset

4. Which word or phrase would NOT be a good replacement for *constantly* in paragraph 12?

a. rarely
b. all the time
c. regularly
d. continually

5. What is the main idea of this chapter?

a. school is boring
b. it's hard to find a good spot for making a video
c. Janey makes her video for her mom's website
d. practice makes perfect

Chapter 5: A Team Effort

1 The activity on Janey's mom's cellphone was ceaseless. All day long she had been receiving calls from friends and neighbors who wanted to congratulate her for being successful at getting the speed limit lowered. Her idea to start a website about the problem had really paid off, and this morning every home on Old Mill Road had received an official letter from the city. The letter was letting them know that in the next few weeks city workers would be putting up signs with the new speed limit: 35 miles per hour.

2 "Gosh, Mom! You're a hero!" Janey exclaimed after her mom finally turned off her phone.

3 "Not really, Janey. I'm just someone who spoke up about a problem that needed to be solved, and I'm only one person. It was all of our neighbors who contacted City Hall about the problem who made the difference. When it was just one person complaining, the city leaders felt like they could ignore me. But they couldn't ignore several dozen people calling and writing. That's what made the difference, not me. Alone, one individual usually can't accomplish much, but when numerous people take action, things change."

4 "Well, Mom, none of that would have happened if you hadn't made the website. People started reading it, and emailing their friends and neighbors, and then they all came to the big meeting you and Dad organized and announced on the website. They took action, but you're the one who helped persuade them to take action. Admit it, Mom – you made it happen! I'm proud of you!"

5 "Well, I guess I can take a little bit of credit," Mom said, "but let's not forget your contribution. The video you made really helped people understand that children are in danger from these cars

zooming past our houses. Many people told me that watching your video is what motivated them to get involved."

6 "So it was a team effort, Mom?"

7 "It certainly was, Janey. You played a big part, and you should be proud of yourself. Your father and I are certainly proud of you."

8 "Thank you, Mom!"

9 "You're very welcome, dear. And I know another team effort you can help me with."

8 "What's that, Mom?"

9 "Eating the pizza your father is picking up on the way home to celebrate our victory."

10 "Eating pizza? That kind of team effort is right up my alley!"

Questions

1. Which word below would NOT be a good replacement for *ceaseless* in paragraph 1?

a. never-ending
b. continuous
c. extremely loud
d. non-stop

2. List two words from paragraph 1 that have four syllables.

____

____

3. Which word would NOT be a good substitute for *contribution* in paragraph 5?

a. share
b. part
c. help
d. name

4. In paragraph 10, Janey says eating pizza is *right up my alley*. What does she mean?

____

____

5. What word in paragraph 1 means to praise someone for something they accomplished?

____

____

POLAR BEARS

1 Polar bears are fascinating creatures. Did you know that they are among the biggest bears in the world? It's true; they're even bigger than grizzly bears. A male polar bear can weigh anywhere from 800 to 1500 pounds, and will be between eight and ten feet long. Here's another fact about polar bears that many people don't know: they spend much of their time in or on the water. In fact, their scientific name is *Ursus maritimus*, which is Latin for "bear of the sea." They are born on land, and they do spend a lot of time on land, but they spend much of their time in the water (or on the ice on top of the water) because their main food source is seals.

Polar Bear

2 Polar bears are only found in areas around the North Pole, and in only five countries: Norway, Canada, Russia, Greenland and the United States (only in Alaska). Their fur is white, which helps them blend in with the snow. This makes it easier to sneak up on seals and catch them, because it's hard for the seals to see them. They also have long snouts and long necks; these help them to look down into holes in the ice over the sea so they can catch seals underwater. Their thick fur allows them to live in an area with very cold temperatures, and their strong claws and teeth are ideal for catching and eating their food. They also have very wide feet. Their big feet and claws allow them to walk on ice without slipping.

Polar Bear Cubs

3 Baby polar bears are born in the winter, between November and February. It's hard to believe how tiny they are at birth. They only weigh about 2 pounds. They are also blind when they're born; their sight develops after they're born. Young polar bears are called cubs. Usually a mother will have two cubs at the same time. They will stay with their mother for around two years before they go out on their own. Most polar bears live for about 20 years.

4 Right now there are about 25,000 polar bears in the world. That might sound like a lot, but it really isn't. Many experts believe that this number is getting smaller every year. Some people are worried that polar bears are going to disappear forever, or go extinct, like wooly mammoths and saber-toothed tigers did. They say that the amount of ice at the North Pole is getting smaller every year. Polar bears need ice in order to survive. Will polar bears go extinct? Let's hope not. Scientists are working hard to prevent this, and we all hope they succeed.

QUESTIONS

1. In paragraph 1, what does *fascinating* mean?

a. moving at high speed
b. very interesting
c. not popular
d. four-legged

2. In paragraph 4, what does succeed mean?

____

____

3. What is the author's purpose of this passage?

a. To persuade
b. To entertain
c. To inform
d. None of the above

4. What is the best summary for this passage?

a. Polar bears are small creatures that live and rely on icy habitats.
b. Polar bears are very large creatures that live and rely on icy habitats.
c. Polar bears are very large creatures that live and rely on warm habitats.
d. Polar bears are small creatures that live and rely on warm habitats.

WALRUSES

Walrus

1 What is the funniest looking animal on earth? Well, there are a lot of funny looking animals in the world, but without a doubt, one of the funniest looking ones is the walrus. They look funny when they're sitting around, they look funny when they're lying down, and they really look funny when they pull themselves out of the water or across the ice by using their long tusks to help them move. In fact, walruses are so funny looking that they're cute! Here's something I bet you didn't know about walruses. Their scientific name is *Odobenus*. That's Latin for "toothwalker."

2 Besides being funny looking, walruses are also huge. They are between eight and twelve feet long, and can weigh nearly 4,000 pounds. They look like gargantuan balls of blubber with two gigantic teeth! In fact, they really are gargantuan balls of blubber – under their skin is a layer of fat that is almost six inches thick. This fat layer is like having a very thick swimsuit on; it keeps them warm in the extremely frigid water where they obtain their food. Their whiskers also contribute to their funny appearance, but they also serve a very important purpose – they help the walrus find its food. Their tusks are around three feet long, and are used for breaking ice, climbing out of the water, and for fighting.

Walrus Whiskers

3 When they're young, walruses have brown skin. It turns lighter and lighter as they age, and the older ones look almost pink. They usually live to be around 25 years old, but some can be as old as 30. Their main foods are small sea creatures such as shrimp, crabs and clam, which they find on the bottom of the sea. They use their whiskers to feel around for food on the sea floor, and they will force creatures out of hiding by spraying a mouthful of water in their direction. They can stay under water for long periods before coming up for air. They can also float for hours at the surface, because they have air bags under their throats.

4 There aren't many animals that eat walruses, which is a good thing, because they are so big they can't move fast enough to get away from a predator. Polar bears and killer whales will attack walruses, but usually they eat young or injured ones. An adult walrus can fight back hard, so killer whales and polar bears prefer to avoid them if they can. All in all, walruses have a pretty sweet life. They get to spend their days swimming in the ocean or lying in the sun, they have all the food they want for free, and the only things they really have to worry about are killer whales and polar bears. Most animals would love to have such an easy life. So walruses might be funny looking, but they're the ones who have the last laugh!

QUESTIONS

1. What does *age* mean in that paragraph?

____

____

2. In paragraph 4, what does *predator* mean?

____

____

3. What is the author's purpose of this passage?

a. To inform
b. To entertain
c. To persuade
d. None of the above

4. What is the best summary for this passage?

a. Walruses are tiny animals with whiskers that live in the Arctic.
b. Walruses are hunted by many different predators.
c. Walruses are large animals with interesting features that live in rivers.
d. Walruses are large animals with unique tusks that live in the Arctic.

Levi Coffin: President of the Underground Railroad

1 Fountain City is a very small town in eastern Indiana. Only about 800 people live in there, but every year, during the third weekend of September, people from all over come to visit Fountain City for the Levi Coffin Days festival. Levi Coffin lived there from 1826 to 1847, and he used his house to hide runaway slaves, and he also helped them get to Canada where they would be free. There were other people back then who also used their houses to hide runaway slaves. Together, these houses were called the Underground Railroad. Levi Coffin helped so many slaves escape that he became known as the President of the Underground Railroad.

Levi Coffin

2 Levi Coffin was born to a Quaker family in North Carolina in 1798. Slavery was legal then, but Quakers were a religious group who disapproved of it. When he was growing up, Levi met many slaves and would often talk to them. He felt sorry for them, and this helped turn him into an abolitionist. An abolitionist was a person who not only disapproved of slavery, but worked to have it outlawed. Many abolitionists also made efforts to help slaves escape. This was against the law, and a person could get into big trouble for helping runaway slaves. Slaves were considered property, and so helping them escape was considered to be stealing from their owner. It also violated the Fugitive Slave Act, which required people to return runaway slaves to their owners. There were people called slave catchers who were paid to capture runaway slaves and bring them back to their owners, and some of them would beat people up for helping slaves escape. So helping slaves escape was not only illegal, but dangerous.

3 Levi Coffin knew that helping slaves escape was illegal and dangerous, but he did it anyway. He hated slavery and wanted to end it. In fact, he hated it so much that he and his wife moved to Indiana, because slavery was illegal there. Back then Fountain City was called Newport, and Levi and his wife bought a farm and opened a general store there. His store was successful, and he began using the money he was making to help runaway slaves. He let other abolitionists know that slaves were welcome to stay at his house. He built secret rooms in his home where they could hide if a

slave catcher showed up looking for them. Then at night he would put them in his wagon, cover them up, and take the slaves to the next house on the Underground Railroad.

Levi Coffin's House

4 Levi Coffin helped more slaves escape than anyone else - over 2,000 slaves spent time in his home over the years. In 1865, after the Civil War, slavery was outlawed in the United States. Levi Coffin died in 1877, so he lived long enough to see his goal of ending slavery fulfilled. Now the house where he hid 2,000 runaway slaves is a National Historic Landmark, and every September, people come to Fountain City to celebrate his life.

Questions

1. Which of the words below means the same thing as *fulfilled* in paragraph 4?

a. destroyed
b. denied
c. ended
d. accomplished

2. In paragraph 2, what is a word that means the same thing as *runaway*?

____

____

3. What word in paragraph 3 means *against the law*?

____

____

4. The word that means *against the law* in paragraph 3 was made by adding a prefix to a base word. What is the base word, and what is the prefix?

____

____

5. Put these events in order of when they took place, by numbering them 1, 2, 3, and 4.

_____: the Civil War

_____: Levi Coffin died

_____: the Underground Railroad started

_____: slavery was outlawed

One Giant Leap for Mankind

1 On July 20, 1969, Neil Armstrong became the first man to walk on the moon, as 500 million people around the world watched on television. This was truly a historic event. Almost all people throughout history would have laughed at the idea that one day a man would walk on the moon. They would have said it was impossible. They would have called a person "crazy" for even talking about the idea. But on July 20, 1969 the man from a small Ohio town proved them wrong.

Neil Armstrong

2 Neil Armstrong was born on August 5, 1930, in Wapakoneta, Ohio. His father had to travel for his job, so the Armstrong family moved about 20 times while Neil was a boy. They moved back to Wapakoneta permanently when he was 14. By this time Neil was in love with flying. Airplanes were still new back then, and most people had never been in one, but Neil took his first plane ride when he was only six years old. He fell in love with flying, and when he was a teenager he started taking flying lessons. He even got a license to fly even before he was old enough to get a driver's license! He was also active in Boy Scouting, and earned its highest rank of Eagle Scout.

3 Neil went off to college at Purdue University in Indiana right after he turned 17. He studied for two years, and then served in the Navy, where he became a fighter pilot. He fought in the Korean War, and then came back to finish his college degree. After college, he joined the Air Force and became a pilot who tested new kinds of aircraft. During his career, he flew in over 200 different kinds of vehicles. It was during this time that the government created NASA to explore space, and in 1962 Neil Armstrong was selected to train as an astronaut.

First Man on the Moon

4 In 1961, President John F. Kennedy had announced that he wanted NASA to land on the moon before 1970. That meant Neil Armstrong and the other astronauts had to work hard to get ready. The work was very dangerous, and some men died while exploring space. Neil Armstrong and the other astronauts bravely continued, though, and Neil was selected to be the first human being to set foot on the moon. After they returned to Earth, he and the other astronauts became national heroes. Neil Armstrong could have used his fame to make a lot of money or run for president, but instead he chose to live a quiet life out of the spotlight, and so he became a college professor. He didn't go on TV or give interviews very often, and he didn't like traveling around giving speeches. He died on August 25, 2012, at age 82. Many people lead remarkable lives, but Neil Armstrong's life was truly "out of this world."

QUESTIONS

1. Why was it a historic event when Neil Armstrong walked on the moon?

____

____

2. In paragraph 4, what is the root word of *bravely*?

____

____

3. Which phrase below means the same thing as *permanently* in paragraph 2?

a. on time
b. before dark
c. for good
d. at the same time

4. What is the best summary for this passage?

a. Neil Armstrong lived a very difficult life after being the first person to walk on the moon.
b. Neil Armstrong's life was quite remarkable as he was the first person to walk on the moon and later became a professor.
c. Neil Armstrong's life was not very interesting even though he went to the moon.
d. Neil Arm strong lived with constant fear of the moon and space after being an astronaut.

Phonics, Language, Grammar, and Word Recognition

Prefixes and Suffixes

PREFIXES

Prefixes are parts of words that are attached to the beginning of root words, which change the meaning of the root word. Take the word *do*, for example. If you add *re-* to *do*, you get *redo*, which means do something again." If your clock is wrong, and you need to set it again, you *reset* it. *Pre-* is also a prefix, which means "before." *Post-* is a prefix which means "after." *Un-* can mean "not", or "opposite." If your friend is not happy, he is *unhappy*. If your neighbor is the opposite of friendly, she is *unfriendly*. *Mis-* means "wrong", so if you aren't paying attention, you might *miscount* the money from your piggy bank. There are lots of different prefixes, but many of them aren't very common. Here is an exercise to help you with some of the prefixes you will see on a regular basis.

For each problem, fill in the blank with the correct answer.

1. If you don't respect someone, you __________ him.

a. unrespect
b. prerespect
c. misrespect
d. disrespect

2. My neighbor mumbles a lot, so I sometimes __________ her.

a. ununderstand
b. disunderstand
c. misunderstand
d. reunderstand

3. Oh, no! The rain washed our sandcastle away, so we will have to ________ it.

a. rebuild
b. postbuild
c. prebuild
d. unbuild

4. That boy is very silly; almost everything he says is __________.

a. unsense
b. nonsense
c. postsense
d. dissense

5. We will have to __________ the frozen turkey before we cook it.

a. refrost
b. unfrost
c. defrost
d. disfrost

6. It's __________ for a person to run faster than a horse.

a. nonpossible
b. unpossible
c. impossible
d. depossible

7. Something that doesn't happen very often is __________.

a. infrequent
b. subfrequent
c. bifrequent
d. overfrequent

8. I don't enjoy cold weather so I __________ winter.

a. inlike
b. dislike
c. unlike
d. relike

9. Do you agree or __________?

a. unagree
b. disagree
c. misagree
d. imagree

10. If your answer was wrong, __________ the problem and try again.

a. overthink
b. unthink
c. disthink
d. rethink

11. It's __________ to drive fast in a schoolzone.

a. unsafe
b. imsafe
c. desafe
d. undersafe

12. The sign says it's __________ to park here.

a. prelegal
b. illegal
c. mislegal
d. translegal

13. A ___________ goes at the beginning of a root word.

a. defix
b. refix
c.misfix
d. prefix

14. Okay, class, let's ___________ what we've learned so far.

a. misview
b. deview
c. review
d. unview

15. If you ___________ cold pizza, it tastes pretty good.

a. reheat
b. misheat
c. unheat
d. deheat

SUFFIXES

Suffixes are like prefixes, except they go on the end of root words. Just like a prefix, a suffix changes the meaning of the root word. With a suffix, *teach* can become *teacher. Kind* can become *kindness. Friend* can become *friendly. Hope* can turn into *hopeless*, or it can turn into *hopeful. Tall* can turn into *taller.* We use many different suffixes every day. Let's practice with them.

For each problem, fill in the blank with the correct answer.

1. I'm sorry to hear about your accident, but I'm very ___________ you weren't hurt.

a. thankness
b. thankly
c. thanker
d. thankful

2. There aren't many choices, so you can't be too ___________.

a. picky
b. pickest
c. pickful
d. pickness

3. Her ___________ under stress helped everyone else relax.

a. calmitude
b. calmless
c. calmness
b. calmy

4. Bill throws a ___________ fastball.

a. powery
b. powerly
c. powerful
d. powerness

5. We're running late, so we have to move ___________.

a. quickful
b. quickly
c. quicky
d. quickless

6. Your cousin from England has a ___________ way of talking.

a. delighter
b. delightness
c. delightly
d. delightful

7. I was so ___________ that I went to bed early.

a. sleepy
b. sleepness
c. sleeper
d. sleeply

8. If we want to win, we have to practice ___________ than ever.

a. hardful
b. hardless
c. harder
d. hardly

9. He doesn't say much, but he's a very ___________ person.

a. thoughtly
b. thoughtful
c. thoughtness
d. thoughty

10. Your painting portrays your dog's face very ___________.

a. niceful
b. niceness
c. niceless
d. nicely

Understanding Latin Suffixes

Many of the words we use in English can be traced back to the language called Latin. Many of the suffixes we use to change the meanings of root words also come from Latin. Here are the most common Latin suffixes:

-able, -ible as in *breakable* or *edible*

-ty, -ity as in *loyalty* or *authority*

-ation as in *location* or *donation*

-fy, -ify as in *notify* or *horrify*

-ment as in *statement* or *pavement*

Draw a line from the word on the right that goes with the definition on the left.

1. kings, queens, princes and princesses	celebration
2. money given to someone for doing something	terrify
3. scare the daylights out of	bendable
4. having nothing to eat for a long time	royalty
5. lights and appliances are powered by this	divisible
6 a big party	electricity
7 able to be bent	admirable
8 swear to tell the truth	testify
9 worthy of being looked up to	payment
10 able to be divided	starvation

Multisyllable Words

Put a slash (/) between syllables in each word below.

Here's an **example:** au/to/mat/ic

1. b o w l i n g
2. p la y g r o u n d
3. b a s k e t b a l l
4. s o c c e r
5. r e f e r e e
6. g y m n a s t
7. g o a l p o s t
8. c a t c h e r
9. o u t f i e l d e r
10. b a s e b a l l
11. q u a r t e r b a c k
12. o v e r t i m e
13. v o l l e y b a l l
14. t u m b l i n g
15. w i n ne r
16. t a c k l e
17. s c o r e b o a r d
18. f u m b l e
19. s t r i k e o u t
20. h o m e r

Spelling Irregular Words

Most of the words we use every day in talking and writing follow regular patterns for spelling, and once you know the patterns, you can figure out how to spell a new word you've just heard. However, not all English words follow these patterns. These words are known as irregular words, and it's good to know them, because they come up a lot. Use the following exercise to improve your spelling of regular words.

Each sentence below has a blank space for a common word. Fill in the blank with the correct spelling from the four choices under each sentence.

1. Sally is my best ________.

a. frend
b. freind
c. friend
d. freand

2. My ________ baked us some cookies for a snack after lunch.

a. moother
b. muther
c. mother
d. muhther

3. Anyone who ________ like to try out can see me after class.

a. wood
b. wude
c. would
d. woold

4. My dad has quite a sense of ________.

a. humor
b. humur
c. humer
c. hughmer

5. There's a lot of work to do, so let's get ________.

a. bussy
b. bizy
c. bizzy
d. busy

6. State your ________ in feet and inches.

a. hite
b. heit
c. heit
d. height

7. You must watch your ________ to keep fit.

a. weight
b. wait
c. wate
d. whate

8. Go ________ to the principal's office, young man!

a. strate
b. straight
c. strait
d. streat

9. The book reports are due by next ________.

a. Wenzday
b. Wednesday
c. Winsday
d. Winsdy

10. They've ________ gone at least a week.

a. ben
b. been
c. bin
d. bean

11. What ________ of books do you like to read?

a. kined
b. kiend
c. kind
d. kynde

12. I need a ________ for my nose.

a. tissue
b. tishue
c. tishoo
d. tissioo

13. Some ________ are taller than men, but most aren't.

a. wimmin
b. wymmin
c. whimmen
d. women

14. Please pass the ________.

a. shooger
b. sugar
c. shugerr
d. shugor

15. I love funny movies because I like to ________.

a. laff
b. lagh
c. lauff
d. laugh

16. If it rains I ________ if we'll be able to finish the game.

a. dout
b. dought
c. doute
d. doubt

17. I ________ a comic book with my allowance.

a. bot
b. bought
c. baught
d. bout

18. My dad started his own ________ right after college.

a. business
b. bizness
c. bisness
d. bisuness

19. Well, Sammy, did you win or ________?

a. loose
b. luze
c. louse
d. lose

20. I'm so hungry I ________ eat a whole pizza!

a. could
b. cood
c. coud
d. cude

Parts of Speech

Fill in the blanks with one of the words in the table below.

Nouns	Adverbs	Adjectives	Verbs	Pronouns

1. ______________________ are words that tell us more about a person, place or thing.

2. ______________________ are words that represent people, places or things.

3. ______________________ are words that show action.

4. ______________________ are words that tell us more about an action.

5. ______________________ are words that take the place of nouns.

Regular and Irregular Plural Nouns

Plural Nouns

With most nouns, it's easy to form a plural by simply adding *–s* to the end of the word. If a word end with a *–y*, change the *–y* to an *–I*, and add *es*. These are called regular nouns. Some nouns don't follow these rules, though. They are called irregular nouns. Let's look at some of them.

If a word ends in *–o*, add *–es*. So *potato* becomes *potatoes*.

If a word ends in *–f*, change the *–f* to *–v* and add *–es*. So *wolf* becomes *wolves*.

If a word ends in *–fe*, change the *–fe* to *–ve* and add *s*. So *knife* becomes *knives*.

Some words don't change, such as *sheep, shrimp* and *deer*. Other words don't really follow any of these rules. For instance, *person* becomes *people*.

Complete the following exercise using your knowledge of regular and irregular verbs. For each question, a singular noun is given. Write the plural form of the noun on the blank line beside it.

1. tornado ______________
2. foot ______________
3. fish ______________
4. elf ______________
5. tomato ______________
6. man ______________
7. calf ______________
8. wife ______________
9. town______________
10. mouse ______________

Concrete Versus Abstract Nouns

A noun is a word that names a person, place, or thing. There are two kinds of nouns. Nouns in the first group are called *concrete nouns*. These words represent something you can see, hear, smell, touch, or taste. Words like *cat, pudding, car, cloud, Tommy, mother, odor, cow, bank*, etc., are concrete nouns. However, some nouns represent things we can't see, hear, touch, taste, or smell. Words like *trust, sacrifice, honor, beauty, truth, obedience, thought, patience*, etc., are called *abstract nouns.*

In each sentence below, one word is underlined. If the word is an abstract noun, write A below the sentence. If the word is a concrete noun, write C below the sentence.

1. When is your birthday?

____

2. The puppy has a lot of energy.

____

3. Please pass the salt.

____

4. Having good health is better than having a lot of money.

____

5. I love reading about history.

____

6. I turned in my report to Mr. Alvarez.

____

7. It takes a lot of discipline to do well at school.

____

8. My cat had five kittens last night.

____

9. My house is three blocks away from the park.

____

10. We all need some help every now and then.

____

Regular and Irregular Verbs

With most verbs, changing from present tense to past tense is easy. All you do is add an *–ed* on the end, or duplicate the last letter of the word, and then add *–ed*. So *walk* becomes *walked*, and *hug* becomes *hugged*. Verbs like this are called regular verbs. Some verbs don't fit into this category, though. They are called irregular verbs.

For each question, use the underlined word in the first sentence to help you write the past tense verb in the blank space of the second sentence.

1. Buy me a hot dog while you're at the concession stand.

Yesterday I _______________ a new comic book with my allowance.

2. Keep the noise down while I'm on the telephone, kids.

I _______________ my sister's hamster in my room while she was at camp.

3. Hang the painting in the center of the wall.

After dinner, the family _______________ ornaments on the Christmas tree.

4. I know a secret.

I _______________ the secret before you did!

5. Class, meet me at the flagpole after the lunch bell rings.

After lunch, we _______________ the teacher at the flagpole.

6. Put the groceries away, Tommy.

I _______________ the groceries away an hour ago, Mom.

7. I go to Eastside Elementary.

I _______________ to the science museum last Saturday.

8. If you want to lose weight, eat fewer snacks.

We _______________ the game by one goal.

9. <u>Bring</u> me your homework, Melissa.

Last year, I _______________ a turtle to class for show and tell.

10. <u>Drink</u> plenty of water on hot days.

Who _______________ the last glass of milk?

Simple Verb Tenses

Verbs are words that show action. The action can be happening right now, or could be in the past, or in the future. We use different forms of verbs to show if a verb is past, present, or future. These forms are called tenses. So *I sing* is present tense, *I sang* is past tense, and *I will sing* is future tense.

In each problem below, two verb tenses are shown, along with a blank line. Fill in the blank with the verb tense that is missing.

1. taste tasted ___________
2. run will run ___________
3. have had ___________
4. kicked kick ___________
5. will talk talked ___________
6. will fly fly ___________
7. sleepwill sleep ___________
8. spoke speak ___________
9. woke will wake ___________
10. will think think ___________

Subject/Verb Agreement

A sentence is always about something. What the sentence is about is called the *subject* of the sentence. In many sentences, the subject is one person, place, or thing. In that case, the subject is singular. In sentences which are about more than one person, place or thing, the subject is plural. Singular subjects must have singular verbs, and plural subjects must have plural verbs. Singular verbs end in *–s* or *–es*. Plural verbs **don't** end in *–s* or *–es*.

PART 1

Use the verbs in the table below to finish the sentences in each question. Make sure the subject and verb agree.

gallop	meows
sings	hold
teach	reads
ring	knows
cuts	drink

1. Mrs. Jones and Ms. Sanchez both ________________ third grade at Eastside Elementary.

2. Santa ________________ if you've been bad or good.

3. Our new cat ________________ when he is hungry.

4. My big sister ________________ in the choir at church.

5. I love to watch the horses ________________ down the pasture.

6. Kids, ________________ your juice and then we'll have dessert.

7. All the bells ________________ at the same time.

8. Every year the teacher ________________ a Halloween party for the entire school.

9. After lunch is over, every student ________________ a book for 15 minutes.

10. Mr. Smith ________________ his lawn at the same time every Saturday.

PART 2

In this passage, several verbs are in bold print. If the verb tense matches the subject, write R above the word (for Right). If the verb tense doesn't match the subject, write W above the word (for Wrong), and then write the correct word.

100,000 Miles a Year

Most people can't **imagine** driving over 100,000 miles in a year. That **are** a lot of driving! In fact, that would be enough miles to get a person almost halfway to the moon. Of course, you can't **drive** to the moon. You would have to fly in a rocket!

The average American **travels** only about 15,000 miles a year in a car. **Think** about your mother and father. If you're like most kids, your parents drive to jobs every day, and they also drive you to school activities. They also **takes** a few other short trips every week.

So who is driving over 100,000 miles a year? Professional truck drivers, that's who. They **goes** between 2000 and 2500 miles every week. It's a good thing they **does**, too. America **depend** on truck drivers. Truck drivers are the heartbeat of our nation's store delivery system. Almost everything people buy at a store was brought there by a truck driver. Truck drivers **makes** our lives much easier and more enjoyable.

Pronoun/Antecedent Agreement

Pretend a friend told you this:

Annette showed me Annette's new bicycle.

That would be very awkward, and it would sound silly. We don't keep repeating the name of a person, place or thing over and over. We use words called pronouns to take their place to avoid sounding awkward. This is how your friend would really tell you about the new bicycle:

Annette showed me her new bicycle.

There are lots of different pronouns. Words like *I, me, we, you, she, him, it, they, them, yours, mine, ours, his, hers,* and *theirs* are all pronouns. Some are singular, and some are plural. Which pronoun to use depends on the word the pronoun is replacing, or referring back to. That word is called the *antecedent*, which means something that comes before something else.

In the sentence above, *Annette* is the antecedent, so the sentence needs a singular pronoun. A singular antecedent needs a singular pronoun, and a plural antecedent needs a plural pronoun. Also, some pronouns are personal pronouns, while others are pronouns that show possession. Words like *I, me, we, you, she, him, he, her, it, they,* and *them* are personal pronouns. Words like *my, mine, yours, his, hers, ours, theirs,* and *its* are possessive pronouns.

Part 1

After each sentence, circle the correct pronoun to fill in the blank.

1. I ate ______ lunch quickly so we could play outside.

my our mine its

2. The band members played ______ instruments perfectly.

yours their its theirs

3. Cindy shared ______ books with her friends.

theirs she they her

4. The cats like sitting in ______ lap.

theirs my its ours

5. If we don't hurry, the game will start without ______.

he she us we

6. Omar has a red backpack, but ______ is blue.

mine my your their

7. Karen got up in front of the class and gave ______ book report.

theirs ours she her

8. Javier said ______ parents grew up in Peru.

him his its theirs

9. The team won ______ last three games.

its mine theirs us

10. Mom told my friends ______ were welcome to stay for supper.

they he she our

Part 2

Match the pronoun on the right by drawing a line to the word or phrase on the left it best fits.

Gabrielle	ours
belongs to him	it
Uncle Bob and Aunt Sally	us
Fred	she
belongs to you and me	theirs
belongs to me	he
you and me	my
belongs to the team	hers
belongs to her	they
the toy	his

Comparative and Superlative Adjectives and Adverbs

ADJECTIVES

Adjectives describe nouns and pronouns. They tell us what kind of person, place or thing something is, like this:

Randy is tall.

The word *tall* tells us something about Randy. Some adjectives can help us compare or contrast different people, places, or things. These are called comparative adjectives and superlative adjectives. Here is a comparative adjective:

Randy is taller than his sister.

The word *taller* tells us something about two different people – Randy and his sister. We use comparative adjectives when discussing two people, places, or things. For comparing more than two, we use superlative adjectives, like this:

Randy is the tallest student in 3rd grade.

When you use comparative and superlative adjectives, there are some easy rules to follow.

For one syllable words, add *–er* to the end for comparative; add *–est* to the end for superlative. (If the adjective ends with *–e*, just add *–r* or *–st*.)

harder softer nicer kindest loudest

If the adjective is only one syllable and the last two letters are a short vowel followed by a consonant, duplicate the consonant and add *–er* or *–est*.

bigger fattest hotter

If the word ends in *–y*, change the *–y* to *–i*, and add *–er* for the comparative, or *–est* for the superlative.

sleepierfuzzier hungrier silliest happiest

For words that have more than one syllable, but don't end in *–y*, use the word *more* in front of it for the comparative; use the words *the most* in front of it for the superlative.

the most wonderful more generous more important the most difficult

There are a few adjectives that don't follow these rules. You probably know these already, because you use them all the time. Here are the two most common ones, along with their comparative and superlative forms:

Good | better | best

Bad | worse | worst

An adjective is listed before each sentence. In each sentence, fill in the blank with the correct form of the adjective, either comparative or superlative. (Answers can be one or two words.)

1. MESSY

My desk is messy, but my closet is even ________________________.

2. FRIENDLY

Heather is the ________________________ girl I know.

3. TALL

Steve is tall, his sister is taller, and his older brother is the ________________________.

4. BAD

This is the ________________________ thunderstorm I've ever seen.

5. HEAVY

This rock is ________________________ than that one.

6. ATHLETIC

I like sports a little, but my brother is ________________________ than I am.

7. SAD

That was the ________________________ story I've ever read.

8. LONG

Which is ________________________, a yard or a meter?

9. ROUGH

Boy, this dirt road is the ________________________ one we've been on so far.

10. BIG

My baby brother is getting ________________________ every day.

Adverbs

Adverbs describe verbs; they tell us how, when, why or where the action took place. Some adverbs don't compare the word to anything else; these are called positive adverbs. Others compare between two actions; these are called comparative adverbs. If an adverb compares three or more actions, it is called a superlative adverb. Here's an example of all three:

Juan ran fast.

Billy ran faster than Juan.

Of the three runners, Cindy was the fastest.

Like many other parts of speech, most comparative and superlative adverbs follow a few basic rules.

In many cases, adverbs end in *–ly*. In these cases, simply put *more* in front of the word for the comparative form, or put *most* in front of the word for the superlative form.

For adverbs that don't end in *–ly*, simply add *–er* or *–est* to the end.

There are a few irregular adverbs that don't follow either of these rules. Here are the main ones, in their positive, comparative and superlative forms.

well *better* *best*

badly *worse* *worst*

In front of each sentence is an adverb. Fill in the blank in each sentence using the correct form of the adverb. Answers can be one or two words.

1. QUICKLY Out of all the students, Joanna came up with the answer ____________________.

2. LOUDLY One cow mooed ____________________ than the other cow.

3. WELL We played well, but unfortunately the other team played ____________________.

4. PROMPTLY Class, this assignment needs to be completed ____________________ than last week's.

5. HARD I worked ____________________ than my brother and got done faster.

6. SLOW Grandpa usually drives ____________________ than Dad does.

7. RAPIDLY All the horses were fast, but Silver Flash galloped the ____________________.

8. EARLY On Saturdays, I always wake up ____________________ than my sister.

9. SOON All three buses left together, but our bus arrived the ____________________ of all.

10. NEATLY Please organize your room ____________________ than you did the last time.

Coordinating and Subordinating Conjunctions

Simple, Compound and Complex Sentences

When it comes to sentence structures, there are three different kinds: simple, compound, and complex. Read this sentence:

I think horses are beautiful.

That's a **simple sentence**. It's called that because it expresses only one idea. That idea is an *independent clause*. It's independent because the idea makes sense all by itself; it's a complete thought.

Here's another sentence:

I think horses are beautiful, and I love to go horseback riding.

That is a **compound sentence**. That means it expresses two ideas, and both of them are independent clauses. To make it easier, just think of this sentence as two simple sentences joined together:

I think horses are beautiful. *I love to go horseback riding.*

A compound sentence always contains a word that joins the two independent clauses together. These words are called coordinating conjunctions. There are only seven coordinating conjunctions: *for, and, nor, but, or, yet, so*. An easy way to remember these is the make-believe word **FANBOYS**; each letter in FANBOYS is the first letter of one of the coordinating conjunctions.

Now look at this sentence:

I think horses are beautiful when they're galloping.

That's a **complex sentence**. It contains an independent clause, and a *dependent clause*. The words *they're galloping* make up a dependent clause – it depends on the rest of the sentence for its meaning. A complex sentence always contains a word or phrase that joins the independent clause to the dependent clause. These are called subordinating conjunctions, and there are many of them. Common ones include *while, after, wherever, where, whenever, unless, though, so that, since, now that, if, how, even though, even if, before, because, as soon as, as long as,* and *although*. The dependent clause can come before the independent clause, or it can come after.

Compound Versus Complex Sentences

Read each sentence and decide if the sentence is a compound sentence, or a complex sentence. Write your answer in the blank space below the sentence.

1. Brian is going to the museum and Wendy is going to the bookstore.

____

2. Although he really didn't want to, Kent agreed to wear a tie to the restaurant.

____

3. After we finish eating, we'll help Mom with the dishes.

____

4. I like pizza a lot, but I also like cheeseburgers.

____

5. If you do a little each day, you will never fall behind.

____

6. Since it's overcast, we had better take our umbrellas.

____

7. Whenever she's hungry, my cat rubs up against my ankles.

____

8. I got an A on my spelling test, and I got a B+ on my vocabulary test.

____

9. We can go to the park, or we can stay here and play.

____

10. Where there's a will, there's a way.

____

Compound Sentences

Each pair of sentences expresses two thoughts, followed by a coordinating conjunction. Rewrite them using one compound sentence, using the coordinating conjunction shown.

1. Fred has the flu. Carol has a cold. AND

____

____

2. I like baseball. I don't like basketball. BUT

____

____

3. You can eat lunch now. You can eat lunch late. OR

____

____

4. You should study hard. You can pass your test. SO

____

____

5. We read about art museums. Our teacher told us about famous painters. AND

____

____

Complex Sentences

Each pair of sentences expresses two thoughts, followed by a subordinating conjunction. Rewrite them using one complex sentence, using the subordinating conjunction shown.

1. The bell rings. It's time for lunch. WHEN

____

____

2. You're not feeling well. You should stay home. IF

____

____

3. You won't get dessert. You eat your vegetables. UNLESS

____

____

4. You must clean your room. You may go outside and play. BEFORE

____

____

5. Watch out for traffic. You ride your bike. WHILE

____

____

Capitalization in Titles

In titles of books, movies, etc, all words should be capitalized, except for the following (unless they are the first or last word in the title): a, an, the, at, by, for, in, of, on, to, up, and, as, but, it, or, nor.

Here are some examples:

- Saved by the Bell
- The Wind in the Willows

Here are ten titles. Follow the rules above to rewrite each one, using proper capitalization.

1. why you should exercise daily

____

2. now they tell me!

____

3. north to alaska

____

4. the hound of the baskervilles

____

5. a tale of two cities

____

6. please don't eat the daisies

____

7. indiana jones and the last crusade

____

8. uncle tom's cabin

____

9. the night before Christmas

____

10. willy wonka and the chocolate factory

____

Commas and Quotation Marks

When you write a city and a state, or a city and a country, you need a comma between them.

Ukiah, California

London, England

Commas are also necessary in dialogue, (when people are talking), along with quotation marks. Look at these sentences:

"Hurry up," Mrs. Smith said, "or you'll be late for school."

Heather said, "That's a lovely hat, Grandmother."

Mrs. Gonzalez asked, "Students, are you ready for the big surprise?"

The commas and quotation marks help us understand what is being said, and help keep us from being confused. Quotation marks always come in pairs, too – one at the beginning of the dialogue being quoted, and one at the end. The last quotation mark should come after the period, question mark or exclamation point.

In the following sentences or addresses, add commas, quotation marks, and other punctuation as needed.

1. Boise Idaho

2. Mom doesn't want us to have snacks before supper Billy reminded Joanie

3. Freida asked What time does the bus usually get here

4. Sir Pedro exclaimed you dropped your wallet

5. Paris France

6. Are those your sunglasses Molly asked

7. James and Kirk said Mr. Brown you need to see me after class

8. Des Moines Iowa

9. Dad said, Let's go to the beach this Saturday

10. I don't think that's a very good idea Mabel her mother replied.

Possessives

Possessives are words that show that something belongs to someone or something, or has a strong relationship with someone or something.

Here are two examples.

That is Bob's bike.

She is Doris's mother.

If the word is a plural, simply add an apostrophe to the end of the word, like this:

The girls' teacher asked them to work on a project together.

The teams' coaches got into a big argument.

The words *my, mine, ours, his, hers, yours, its, their,* and *their* s are also possessives.

Each sentence below sounds awkward. Rewrite each one using a possessive, as in the example shown.

This ball belongs to them.

This is their ball. ___________

1. Let's say hello to the mom of Tanequa.

____

____

2. This is the uniform that belongs to Jack.

____

____

3. I rode the new bike that belongs to Freddy.

____

____

4. Here's the bib that belongs to the baby.

____

____

5. The stall that belongs to the horse needs cleaned.

____

____

6. Here's the book that belongs to you.

____

____

7. This is the new video game that belongs to Charles.

____

____

8. The bus that you ride is coming.

____

____

9. The dog wagged the tail that belongs to the dog.

____

____

10. The fingers of the boys were freezing after they built the snowman.

____

____

High Frequency Words

Unscramble the mixed up high frequency word in each problem and write it in the blank below.

1. A talking fish? That's mispsiboel!

____

2. I'll have to ask my parents, but I bporably will be able to attend your birthday party.

____

3. Okay, vebreoydy, we need to keep the noise down.

____

4. I hope the awtehre is nice when we go camping.

____

5. Don't litter – help keep America aebutiufl.

____

6. All the dresses on sale look nice, but this one's the petirtets.

____

7. We all alehdug at the funny clown.

____

8. Students, don't yell. Raise your hand if you have a utesoqni.

____

9. We practiced every day ebaucse we wanted to win.

____

10. In what year did Columbus idcrsove America?

____

Base Words and Suffixes

We can add a suffix to many words to make a new word. Some of these suffixes are *-ion, -ment, -ing, -y, -al, -ive, -est, -ation, -ed, -ation, -able, -ly, -ful, -ment,* and *-less*. If the base word end in a silent-*e*, and the suffix begins with a vowel, drop the –*e*. This includes suffixes that start with –*y*.

Add a suffix to the base word listed in front of each sentence to make a new word to complete the sentence.

1. SCARE Boy, those stories around the campfire were really ____________________.

2. EXCITE That was the most ____________________ basketball games I've ever seen.

3. INTEREST I'm sorry, but I just didn't find the book to be very ____________________.

4. REPLACE Class, Ms. Brown is sick today, so I will be her ____________________.

5. NEW These are the ____________________ versions; they just came out.

6. HOPE It's ____________________; we'll never dig a hole to China at this rate.

7. MUD My boots were really ____________________ after our hike in the rain.

8. ACCIDENT I didn't do it on purpose; it was ____________________.

9. HAPPY Working in his garden brings Grandpa much ____________________.

10. MUSIC There are nearly 50 ____________________ in the marching band.

Word and Phrase Choice

There are many ways of talking or writing about similar things, using different words. Some words have almost the same meaning as other words, but leave a different impression on the listener or reader. You can choose what effect to have on the reader or listener by choosing which words to use. Let's practice.

For each problem, there will be three choices. Circle the one that is the best choice.

1. If someone asked you how you felt about a test coming up in ten minutes, and you weren't ready at all, and you were pretty sure you were going to fail, what would be the best way to phrase it to make your feelings clear?

a. I'm anxious.
b. I'm nervous.
c. I'm worried.

2. Which of these sentences is the most appropriate?

a. In the middle of a daydream, Becky was startled by the classroom bell.
b. In the middle of a daydream, Becky was shocked by the classroom bell.
c. In the middle of a daydream, Becky was terrified by the classroom bell.

3. Which sentence best expresses the idea that a comedian was extremely funny?

a. The comedian was humorous.
b. The comedian was hilarious.
c. The comedian was amusing.

4. Which of these sentences gives the right effect?

a. I thought I would die chuckling.
b. I thought I would die snickering.
c. I thought I would die laughing.

5. How would a person who can hardly believe how tall and heavy an elephant is try to communicate its size to someone else?

a. The elephant was large.
b. The elephant was huge.
c. The elephant was big.

6. If you loved to play in the snow, what would your reaction be if you woke up one day to find a foot of snow outside?

a. This is nice.
b. This is neat.
c. This is wonderful.

7. If you saw a car go by your house at a high rate of speed, which of these sentences would be the best way to describe it?

a. The car went past my house.
b. The car streaked past my house.
c. The car drove past my house.

8. Which of these sentences sounds nicest?

a. Oh, what an obese little baby!
b. Oh, what an overweight little baby!
c. Oh, what a chubby little baby!

9. Which of these sentences sounds the least like boasting?

a. We defeated the other team.
b. We trounced the other team.
c. We destroyed the other team.

10. Which sentence is the best for describing the story of Paul Bunyan and Babe?

a. It is a tall tale.
b. It is a lie.
c. It is a falsehood.

Spoken and Written English

The rules we follow when we talk are different than the rules we use when writing. Writing is considered to be formal, while talking is informal, or relaxed. Slang is fine when we're talking with friends, but is not acceptable in letters to people we don't know well. When we talk, we use lots of contractions, such as *don't, can't, didn't, shouldn't,* etc. When writing, these are frowned upon, except in writing dialogue, or penning a note or letter to a good friend. When we're talking, we can use our voice and our body language to communicate, as well as our words, so we don't need to be quite as exact in our phrasing. In writing, we can only use words and punctuation to get our message across, so we need to be more precise when choosing our words.

Read each sentence, and decide if it's more appropriate as a spoken sentence, or a written sentence. Write S for spoken or W for written on the line next to the sentence.

1. Who was that dude I saw you talking to? _______

2. The weather forecast for Saturday does not sound promising for our picnic. _______

3. I would like to return the item I purchased and request a refund. _______

4. That'll teach 'em! _______

5. What's up? _______

6. Whatever you say, pal! _______

7. I am expressing my strong disapproval of the ordinance which has been proposed._______

8. Refreshments will be provided. _______

9. What's up with that?_______

10. We would like to invite you to come visit us at Christmas. _______

Root Words

Each sentence has one underlined word, which contains a prefix or a suffix. Use your knowledge of the root word to figure out the definition of the new word, and circle the correct answer.

1. Being near a loud siren can be very unpleasant.

a. fun
b. enjoyable
c. not enjoyable

2. If you are overconfident, you may fail the test.

a. not confident enough
b. having too much confidence
c. a little confident

3. Charles Lindbergh made the first solo transatlantic flight.

a. across the Atlantic Ocean
b. into the Atlantic Ocean
c. under the Atlantic Ocean

4. My little brother gets hyperactive when he eats too much sugar.

a. not active
b. less active
c. very active

5. After his team won the game, Jack became boastful.

a. not boasting very much
b. not boasting at all
c. boasting a lot

6. Teresa is the most unfriendly person I know.

a. not friendly
b. very friendly
c. popular

7. Don't let one bad grade discourage you.

a. give lots of courage
b. take away courage
c. give a little more courage

8. You acted honorably, Sandy.

a. in an honorable way
b. not in an honorable way
c. in a confused way

9. We must preheat the oven for fifteen minutes.

a. heat the oven after putting the food in
b. heat the oven before putting the food in
c. heat the oven while the food is in

10. The snowfall made for a <u>wondrous</u> sight the next morning.

a. ugly
b. boring
c. full of wonder

Suffix and Prefix Additions

Using a suffix or prefix, fill in the blank with letters to change the word to match the definition shown.

1. not agree = __________agree

2. not believable = __________believable

3. state of being happy = happ__________

4. do again = __________do

5. not polite = __________polite

6. in a quick manner = quick__________

7. state of being aware = aware__________

8. person who teaches = teach__________

9. having a magic quality = magic__________

10. possessing caution = cauti__________

Figurative Language

SIMILES

A simile is a phrase that compares two things and uses the words *like* or *as*.

Example: That child is as wiggly as a worm.

METAPHORS

A metaphor is a word or phrase to compare two things <u>without</u> using the words *like* or *as*.

Example: His brain is a computer.

PERSONIFICATION

Personification is when human qualities or characteristics are given to something that is not human. This can be an object, animal, or abstract idea.

Example: The tree branch tapped on the glass.

HYPERBOLE

A hyperbole is an extreme exaggeration to emphasize a point. It is not generally meant to be taken literally.

Example: I am so hungry that I could eat a horse.

Read the sentences below, and indicate whether they are examples of similes, metaphors, personification, or hyperboles.

1. The flowers danced happily in the wind. ______________________

2. The chocolate cream pie was smooth as silk. ______________________

3. The store was as busy as a group of working ants.

____

4. My purse weighs a ton. ______________________

5. The sun smiled warmly at me. ______________________

6. I am drowning in paperwork. ______________________

7. Time is money. ______________________

8. The wind howled on the cold and blustery day. ______________________

9. Warren's heart is gold. ______________________

10. She cried so long that she made a lake with her tears.

____

Practice Test #1

Questions 1 – 11 pertain to the following passage:

MIGUEL'S WORLD

Old Logs Help Animals

Miguel Gonzalez and his father took many walks in the woods near their house. When Miguel was very young, around five, he liked to pick up branches and hit them against the ground and the trees. Sometimes he would waive the stick and pretend he was fighting a great battle. Mr. Gonzalez always told Miguel to drop the stick.

"You will poke an eye out," said Mr. Gonzalez. A few years later, Miguel stopped hitting with sticks and started asking his father about the trees and other things he saw in the woods. Miguel's father told him how to identify different trees by the texture of their bark and the size and shape of their leaves. Miguel found out how trees spread their seeds and what kinds of animals eat the leaves, bark, and seeds. Miguel loved taking walks with his father, but he did not appreciate all the things that he saw in the woods. One day they almost tripped over a log that had fallen on the trail. Miguel kicked it.

"Stupid log, it almost made me fall," he said. Miguel's father waved his arms, shook his head, and told his son to stop.

"That's not just a piece of wood, Miguel," said Mr. Gonzalez. "That log is a home for many creatures and plants. Kicking that log would be like an earthquake to them! How would you like it if a giant ant kicked our house?"

"There are ants in there?" asked Miguel.

"Watch," said Mr. Gonzalez. He brushed the old brown leaves and rotting bark off the top of the log until they could see the wood buried underneath. On the smooth surface were clusters of small dark holes. An ant poked its head from one of the holes. Miguel laughed.

"Is there anything else in that log?" Miguel asked.

"Let's see," said Mr. Gonzalez. The two brushed off more leaves. They worked carefully to avoid touching the slimy slugs that dotted the log. Near the end of the rotten piece of timber was a large rough hole. A squirrel darted out from the hole and chattered noisily. On the nearby trees, birds called and sang noisily, too.

"They're waiting for us to leave so they can eat," smiled Mr. Gonzalez. "Those ants and slugs may not seem tasty to us, but they are a gourmet treat for the birds."

"Let's go," said Miguel. "They look hungry, and I hate making them wait for lunch." After a few minutes, Miguel turned suddenly and started walking quickly in the opposite direction, back toward the log.

"Hey, what are you doing? What's up?" called Miguel's father.

Miguel stopped and turned around. "We left the log uncovered. If we don't put the leaves and bark back where we found them, the ants won't have anywhere to hide."

Miguel's father laughed and started to jog toward his son. "A little while ago you hated that log. Now you want to protect it."

"You always told me, treat others as you want to be treated," said Miguel with a smile. "I'm just following your advice!"

1. Paragraph 1 is mostly about:

a. The woods near Miguel's house
b. Miguel's father's love for nature
c. Miguel's behavior during walks
d. How sticks can be used as weapons

2. How did Miguel change when he got older?

a. He became more frightened of the woods
b. He became more dangerous toward his father
c. He became more bored with his father
d. He became more interested in the woods

3. Which meaning best fits the way the word "identify" is used in paragraph 2?

a. To become the same
b. To understand well
c. To recognize
d. To symbolize

4. What is a central theme of the story?

a. Selfishness
b. Empathy
c. Heroism
d. Independence

5. How does the theme develop throughout the story?

a. The theme shifts from ignorance to empathy.
b. The theme shifts from selflessness to selfishness.
c. The theme shifts from dependence to independence.
d. The theme shifts from weakness to heroism.

6. How does Mr. Gonzalez's character develop throughout the story?

a. He became mean and arrogant.
b. He became very sad instead of happy.
c. He became more of an empathizer than a guide.
d. He became more of an observer rather than a teacher.

7. How can Miguel's journey in nature be seen as a metaphor for maturing?

a. Miguel recognized the need to take responsibility for his actions.
b. Miguel realized he didn't belong in the woods.
c. Miguel did not need to listen to his dad anymore.
d. Miguel understood that he was not the only living thing in the woods.

8. Read the chart below. It shows the order in which some events happened in the story.

Miguel played with sticks during walks in the woods with his father.
⇩
⇩
Miguel and his father walk away so the birds can eat the ants and slugs in the log.
⇩
Miguel runs back to the log to put the leaves and bark back on top of the log.

Which of the following statements belongs in the empty box?

a. Miguel's father tells him not to kick the log.
b. Miguel laughs at the ants.
c. Miguel gets angry and goes home.
d. Miguel's father sits on the log.

9. Which sentence from the story showed that Miguel changed his mind?

a. "You always told me, treat others as you want to be treated"
b. "A little while ago you hated that log. Now you want to protect it."
c. "They look hungry, and I hate making them wait for lunch."
d. "If we don't put the leaves and bark back where we found them, the ants won't have anywhere to hide."

10. The golden rule is to treat others the way you want to be treated. In what ways does the story reflect the golden rule?

a. Miguel kicking the log.
b. Miguel's reaction to the log being in his way.
c. Miguel's change in attitude towards nature.
d. Miguel's initial lack of empathy towards the creatures living in the log.

11. How does Mr. Gonzalez play a role in Miguel's character development?

a. Mr. Gonzalez instructs Miguel to put the leaves back the way they were.
b. Mr. Gonzalez encourages independent thinking and self-reflection through accountability.
c. Mr. Gonzalez gets mad at Miguel for his selfish behaviors.
d. Mr. Gonzalez guides Miguel to fix his mistakes.

Questions 12 – 17 pertain to the following passage:

The Best Friend I Found

My name is Tanya, and I have a dog whose name is Maize. I found her one summer in the parking lot of a supermarket when she was a puppy. I was taking our cart back to the store when I saw a small black and white animal dart under a row of shopping carts next to the main door. It moved so fast, all I saw was a blur. I did not know if the animal was a cat, a dog, or a skunk until it started barking.

My mom always told me not to play with strange animals, but something about Maize seemed safe. I bent down to find her under the carts and called to her. She came creeping out, slowly at first. Then she ran straight to me, wagging her tail. I picked her up and brought her back to my mom.
"Look what I found!" I said, holding up Maize, as she licked my face.
"No," said my mom.

I was about to protest when the puppy leaned over to my mom and licked her hand. Then she tried to lick my mom's face. My mom started to laugh.

"You are cute!" she said to the puppy. "It's hard to say no to a kiss like that."

"Can we keep her?" I asked.

"If you take care of her," said Mom. "You have to feed her, take her out for walks, and train her to behave."

At first, I was excited to have a dog. Maize slept on my bed and woke me up every morning by jumping on my bed. I took her for long walks in the park. Then school started, and I had to wake up early to take Maize outside before I got on the bus. I had to fill her food and water bowls as soon as I got home. I could not go to my friends' houses because I had to be home to take care of Maize. I started to wish I had not found Maize.

One Friday afternoon I was walking down my street when I saw my best friend, Laticia.

"Hey Tanya!" Laticia called. "Is that Maize?"

"Yes," I said.

"Wait here," said Laticia. "I am going to ask my mom if I can come over to play with you guys."

After a few minutes, Laticia came back. "Mom said I can come over for an hour, so let's go," she said.

We had a great time—Laticia, Maize, and me. Now my friends come over to my house to play all the time. They want to see me and play with Maize. I'm so glad I found Maize. She's the best friend a girl could have.

12. What do you think "dart" means?

a. a sharp pointed object
b. an animal
c. a quick movement
d. to hide under something

13. Which one of these sentences from the story is a hyperbole?

a. "She's the best friend a girl could have."
b. "You have to feed her, take her out for walks, and train her to behave."
c. "One Friday afternoon I was walking down my street when I saw my best friend, Laticia."
d. "She came creeping out, slowly at first."

14. What is the main problem in the story?

a. Tanya's mom won't let her keep Maize
b. Tanya's friends don't like Maize
c. Maize is messing up the house during the day
d. Tanya can't visit her friends after school

15. How did Laticia solve Tanya's problem?

a. Laticia went over to Tanya's house
b. Tanya went to Laticia's house
c. Tanya gave Maize away
d. Tanya and her mom went to the supermarket

16. What sentence best summarizes this story?

a. Tanya is given a puppy as a present, but she doesn't like having to take care of it all the time.
b. Tanya finds a puppy in the grocery parking lot, and, regardless of initial challenges, she grows to love the puppy as her new friend and companion.
c. Tanya finds a puppy, but she is so focused on her friends, she neglects the puppy.
d. Tanya is given a puppy, and the puppy helps her make a lot of new friends.

17. How does Tanya change throughout the story?

a. Tanya immediately found a best friend, but then she became sad when she had to take care of the dog.
b. Tanya disliked the dog, and then she began to feel bad and sympathize for the dog.
c. Tanya was very overwhelmed trying to care for the dog, but she eventually grew to love and value the relationship she had developed.
d. Tanya was excited about the dog at first, but then she became overwhelmed and wished she had never found the dog in the first place.

Questions 18 – 24 pertain to the following passage:

The Animal Times

Bats Our Flying Friends by Martha Gold

Most people are afraid of bats. They are scared of their sharp teeth. They are scared because bats only come out at night. People worry that bats will bite them, but bats do not feed on people. Most bats in North America eat insects that they catch in the air with their teeth. Some bats eat mice, birds, frogs, lizards, and other bats. One kind of bat in Mexico catches fish in the claws of its hind legs. In Asia, large bats called Flying Foxes eat fruit. Other bats with long noses drink sweet juice from flowers.

All bats are mammals. They are the only mammals that fly. Bats live everywhere in the world except Antarctica and the North Pole. Most bats do not drink blood. Only vampire bats drink blood. Vampire bats live in Central and South America. They land on animals and bite them to make a tiny cut. Then they lap up the blood with their tongues. Vampire bats rarely bite people. If they do bite, they do not take much blood. However, bats may carry germs that cause disease.

Bats are not good pets, but they are useful to people. They eat insects, mice and other pests. Some cultures even think bats bring good luck!

18. What is the central idea of the passage?

a. People don't like bats because they are harmful to people.
b. Bats are cool creatures.
c. Bats are beneficial to people, but they are often misunderstood.
d. Bats are harmful to ecosystems, but many people are intrigued by them.

19. What piece of evidence from the text does not help support the central idea?

a. "Bats are not good pets, but they are useful to people."
b. "All bats are mammals."
c. "People worry that bats will bite them, but bats do not feed on people."
d. "Most people are afraid of bats."

20. What is the author's purpose of the text?

a. To inform
b. To persuade
c. To entertain
d. None of the above

21. What piece of evidence from the text could the author use to best support the claim that bats help the ecosystem?

a. "Most bats in North America eat insects that they catch in the air with their teeth."
b. "However, bats may carry germs that cause disease."
c. "Bats live everywhere in the world except Antarctica and the North Pole."
d. "They land on animals and bite them to make a tiny cut."

22. Look at the diagram below about flying foxes and vampire bats, and then answer the question that follows.

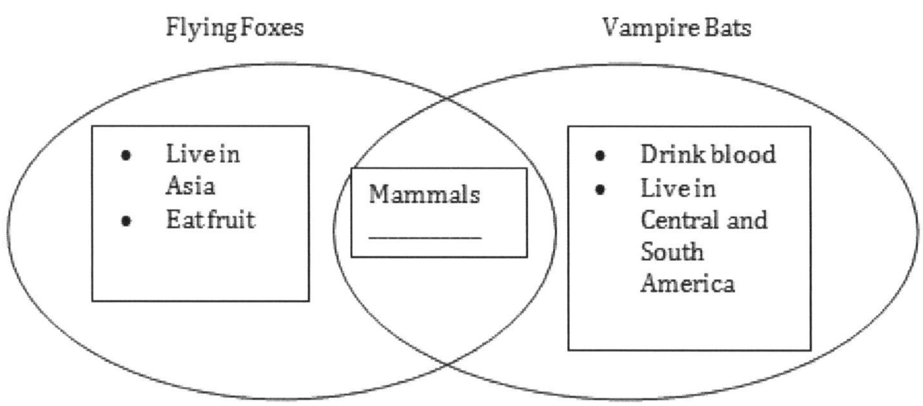

Which of the following belongs in the blank?

a. Bite animals and sometimes people
b. Eat insects
c. Make good pets
d. Only come out at night

23. What does the word "disease" mean in the last sentence of the second paragraph?

a. an injury
b. abnormal growth changes in the body that happen during fetal development
c. an immune overreaction by the body to a substance
d. an illness or sickness

24. What does the title infer about the passage?

a. Bats should become pets.
b. Bats can understand our feelings.
c. Bats are helpful and not harmful to humans.
d. Bats can bring humans happiness.

Questions 25 -31 pertain to the following passage:

Sam, My Teddy Bear

When I was just a child of three, I got a teddy bear.
With a squeeze, I called him Sam, and I took him everywhere,
To my grandma's, the babysitter's, the doctor's, and the pool.
Sometimes big kids would laugh at me, but my friends thought Sam was cool.
But all that travel took its toll on Sam's good looks.
His fur wore off in patches and his ears bent into crooks.
Now he stays put on a shelf,
Next to some blocks and a small green elf.
I still love Sam and would never give him away,
but I'm too old for teddy bears, so in my room he'll stay.

25. What choice best summarizes this poem?

a. Sam wore out after a few years. His fur was in patches and his ears were bent. He looked old
b. A girl got a teddy bear for a present and took it everywhere. Then she got bored with it
c. A girl got a teddy bear for a present and loved it. After taking it everywhere with her, she outgrew it, but she still loves it
d. The girl took the bear everywhere, to her grandmother's, the babysitter's and the pool. Kids laughed at her

26. What kind of poem is this?

a. Free verse
b. Rhymed verse
c. Haiku
d. Limerick

27. What is the theme of the poem?

a. Reflecting on "the good old days"
b. Solving a conflict
c. Experiencing romantic love
d. Depicting an identity crisis

28. How does the narrator develop throughout the poem?

a. The narrator began to hate Sam since older children made fun of Sam.
b. The narrator eventually realized the necessity of Sam.
c. The narrator realized that Sam was just a silly toy.
d. The narrator eventually outgrew the need to carry Sam everywhere.

29. How does the narrator's perspective of Sam change?

a. The narrator still values Sam, but he no longer idolizes him.
b. The narrator feels the need to take Sam everywhere.
c. The narrator thinks Sam is just a silly, old toy.
d. The narrator thinks Sam makes him uncool.

30. What does the word "crooks" mean in the poem?

a. Thieves
b. Hooked staffs
c. Shape or curve
d. Dishonest people

31. What is the correct order of events in this poem?

a. Child receives Sam. Child takes Sam everywhere. Child puts Sam on a shelf
b. Child puts Sam on a shelf. Child takes Sam everywhere. Child receives Sam
c. Child takes Sam everywhere. Child receives Sam. Child puts Sam on a shelf
d. Child receives Sam. Child puts Sam on a shelf. Child takes Sam everywhere

Questions 32 – 40 pertain to the following passage:

Fire Needs Fuel and More to Burn

On the ground lay a dead tree, its branches sticking out like a porcupine's quills. Jake started breaking off the branches and putting them in a pile. His father had sent him to find kindling wood for their fire.

"What's kindling wood?" Jake asked.

"Boy! You've been living in the city too long, Jake!" said Jake's father. "Kindling is little branches no thicker around than this." He held up his hand and made a circle with his first finger and thumb. "We need them to start the fire."

Jake measured the circumference of the branches by wrapping his first finger and thumb around each one. If the thumb and finger touched, he put it in the pile. If his finger and thumb could not touch, he left it on the tree. After he had collected an armful, Jake brought the pile of branches to his father.

His father was crumpling newspaper and arranging it around the cement circle that held up an iron grill. The wood was dry, brown, and old, but not rotten.

"Perfect kindling, Jake," said his father. "Good job!"

He piled the kindling on top of the newspapers and lit a match. The flames crept up the corners and edges of the paper and curled around the sticks. Soon the flames were flickering, and Jake's father put on the first log.

"What makes fire burn?" asked Jake, as he set out plates and cups on the picnic table for dinner.
"Three things," said his father. "I'll give you a hint. You are breathing one of them right now."

"Smoke?" asked Jake, coughing.

"Oxygen," said Jake's father, laughing. "The wood we're using is another. Wood is fuel, paper is fuel, and gasoline is fuel. Anything that can burn is fuel. Finally, you need high heat, called the kindling temperature, so the fuel will catch fire and make flames."
"How hot does the kindling temperature have to be?" asked Jake.

"It's different for different kinds of fuel," said Jake's father. "For wood it is about 500ºF (260ºC). Some fuels need a higher kindling temperature, and some need a lower temperature."

Jake looked down at the fire. The flames crept around the log and started to catch on to the bark. The flames flickered around the iron bars, but the bars did not burn.

"Why doesn't the iron in the grill burn?" asked Jake.

"It's fireproof," said Jake's father. "Oxygen cannot mix with it, so it cannot burn. It is the same with stone or brick."

"It's a good thing," said Jake, as he unwrapped the hotdogs. "Or we would have to order out for pizza!"

32. What is the main idea of the passage?

a. Jake learned about the essential components of making a fire.
b. Jake got to spend quality time with his dad.
c. Jake learned about what kinds of trees are safe for making fires.
d. Jake learned how to make dinner.

33. In the second paragraph, what does the word "circumference" mean?

a. The distance around a circle
b. The distance across a circle
c. The distance across a stick
d. The distance along a stick

34. What is the theme of the passage?

a. Friendship
b. Learning and discovery
c. Perseverance
d. Empathy

35. How does Jake change throughout the passage?

a. Jake decides to become a fireman when he grows up.
b. Jake becomes arrogant about his skills.
c. Jake loses his curiosity about fire.
d. Jake becomes more knowledgeable about fire.

36. What is the order of events in this story?

a. Jake takes out hotdogs. Jake gets kindling wood. Jake's father starts the fire
b. Jake's father starts the fire. Jake takes out hotdogs. Jake gets kindling wood
c. Jake's father starts the fire. Jake gets kindling wood. Jake takes out hotdogs
d. Jake gets kindling wood. Jake's father starts the fire. Jake takes out hotdogs

37. How does Jake's perspective differ from his father's perspective in the story?

a. Jake's perspective is practical while his father's is curious and eager to learn.
b. Jake's perspective sees the task as routine yet his father's is unfamiliar with the task.
c. Jake's perspective lacks experience and knowledge compared to his father's.
d. Jake's perspective comes from the position of a teacher whereas his father's comes from the position of a learner.

38. Which of these sentences from the passage displays personification?

a. "He piled the kindling on top of the newspapers and lit a match."
b. "The flames crept up the corners and edges of the paper and curled around the sticks."
c. "Oxygen cannot mix with it, so it cannot burn."
d. "If the thumb and finger touched, he put it in the pile."

39. What is the best summary of this passage?

a. A young boy, Jake, learns how to gather small pieces of wood to start a fire with his father's guidance and support.
b. A young boy, Jake, teaches his father how to gather small pieces of wood to start a fire.
c. A young boy, Jake, explores and plays with fire with his friends.
d. A young boy, Jake, learns how to gather small pieces of wood and start a fire in his boy scouts group.

40. In paragraph 7, what does the word "flickering" mean?

a. Slowly dying or losing energy
b. Shining or radiating brightly
c. Wavering or fluttering with quick, irregular motions
d. Steady and constant light

Practice Test #2

Questions 1 – 9 pertain to the following passage:

Snacks Made Easy By Martha Gold

After school, Mika came running from the school bus into her house.

"Mom, I'm starving," she said, dropping her school bag on the kitchen floor and opening the refrigerator. "What do we have to eat?"

"Not much," said her mother. "I have to go shopping today."

"Do we still have those cheese crackers?" asked Mika.

"We're all out," said Mika's mother. "If you want, we can make some."

"MAKE them?" asked Mika. "You mean with cheese and stuff?"

"There is a recipe I want to try," said Mika's mother. "Why don't we make some? Then we can go shopping."

"But I want something NOW," whined Mika.

"Have some fruit," said her mother, holding out an apple.

"Okay," said Mika, taking the apple. "Now, how do you make these crackers?"

Mika's mother put a sheet of paper on the kitchen table in front of her. On the paper was a recipe, or directions, on how to make cheese crackers.

Cheese Crackers

Ingredients:

1-cup all-purpose flour and a little
Extra flour to roll out dough
1/2-teaspoon salt
4 tablespoons cold butter
8 ounces grated cheese
(Cheddar or Monterey Jack)
1/4-cup of water

Cooking Utensils:
1 large mixing bowl
1 measuring cup
1/2-teaspoon measure
Mixing spoon
Rolling pin
Cookie cutters
2 table knives or potato masher

Directions:

1. Heat the oven to 350° F.
2. Cut the butter into small pieces.
3. Mix the flour and salt together in a large bowl.
4. Add the butter and cut it into the flour using two table knives or a potato masher. Cut until the pieces of butter are smaller than a pea.
5. Add the water gradually, one tablespoon at a time. Mix it in until the dough sticks together in a ball.
6. Cover the bowl with plastic wrap. Put it in the refrigerator for half-an-hour.
7. Sprinkle flour on a clean table or on the counter. Put the dough in the middle of the flour.
8. Roll out the dough until it is as thick as a regular-sized magazine. Cut out shapes using small cookie cutters.
9. Place the shapes on a greased, non-stick cookie sheet. Bake for 15 minutes, or until the crackers are golden brown. Let cool and enjoy!

1. What is the author's purpose of this selection?

a. To explain
b. To persuade
c. To entertain
d. None of the above

2. What is the best summary of this passage?

a. Mika is too hungry to wait and make crackers.
b. Mika wants to learn how to be a chef.
c. Mika and her mother follow a recipe to make cheese crackers.
d. Mika prefers homemade cheese crackers over store bought ones.

3. What step must happen first when following the recipe?

a. Cover the bowl with plastic wrap.
b. Put the dough in the middle of the flour.
c. Cut out shapes using small cookie cutters.
d. Sprinkle flour on a clean table or on the counter.

4. What does the word "ingredient" mean?

a. A statement that tells how to do something
b. One of the items used to make a food.
c. The temperature at which the food should bake
d. A name for the recipe

5. How did Mika's mom fix her problem of wanting food immediately?

a. She went and bought her crackers from the gas station.
b. She gave her an apple to eat while they make the crackers.
c. She told her to be patient for the crackers to be done.
d. She gave her some money to go to the store herself to get something.

6. Which of the following meanings best fits the way "gradually" is used in step 5?

a. A little at a time
b. Slowly
c. Not steep
d. Continuously

7. How does Mika change throughout the story?

a. Mika was impatient, and she ended up getting mad at her mom.
b. Initially, Mika was patient, but as they were cooking, she became impatient and was complaining.
c. At first Mika is impatient and complaining, but then her attitude shifts to as she is willing to wait and learn.
d. At first Mika wanted to make the crackers, but then she got discouraged thinking it was too difficult to do.

8. Which answer should go in the blank?

What Happens	Why It Happens
Mika read the cheese crackers recipe.	________________________

a. Mika wants to make cheese crackers
b. Mika wants to go shopping
c. Mika wants another apple
d. Mika wants a different snack

9. Which of the following sentences from the selection is a hyperbole?

a. "Mika's mother put a sheet of paper on the kitchen table in front of her."
b. "Mix it in until the dough sticks together in a ball."
c. "Mom, I'm starving."
d. "After school, Mika came running from the school bus into her house."

Questions 10 – 18 pertain to the following passage:

An Unforgettable Day at the History Museum by Martha Gold

1. Hakeem's third-grade class takes a field trip every spring to the county historical museum. The county historian gives the class a tour and afterward sets the students loose to explore the museum. Hakeem's older brother, Gerard, went two years earlier. Gerard said the museum was great except for one room.

"Watch out for the room with the old war uniforms, it's haunted," said Gerard at dinner one night.

"What do you mean, haunted?" asked Hakeem.

2. "We heard funny noises in the room," said Gerard. "We looked around to see if anyone else was there, but it was empty. Then Sammy swore he saw the eyes of one of the costume dummies move around, as if it were watching us. We were so scared we left before we got to the end of the exhibit."

"Gerard, stop scaring your brother," said Hakeem's mother. "Hakeem, there is no such thing as ghosts. I'm sure there is a logical explanation for those noises. As for the eyes moving, that's just Sammy's imagination getting out of hand."

3. Stories about ghosts usually do not frighten Hakeem. He laughed at all the ghost stories his counselor told at camp last summer around the campfire. He watched scary movies with his babysitter and felt fine. But something about Gerard's words made Hakeem feel uneasy. Gerard does not usually joke around. Hakeem doubted that Gerard was just trying to scare him. Instead, Gerard was probably trying to warn him.

4. On the day of the field trip, Hakeem asked his teacher, Mr. Orwell, about Gerard's story as they rode the bus to the museum.

"It's an old building," said Mr. Orwell. "The floor boards creak and I'm sure there are other parts of the museum that make strange noises. It's not haunted, just a little creepy."
"What about the eyes watching Sammy?" asked Hakeem.

Mr. Orwell laughed. "Sammy's got a great imagination," he said. "I'm sure that's what made him think the statue was watching him."

5. After the tour, Hakeem walked around the museum with his best friend Malcolm. Malcolm wanted to see the old war uniforms, but Hakeem was nervous. Finally, he agreed to follow his friend into the room. There were just a few standing lamps and one small bulb on the ceiling to provide light. Ten life-size dummies, or mannequins, each one wearing a different war uniform, stood in the dim room. As Hakeem walked by a mannequin, the overhead light flickered. At that moment, Hakeem looked at the mannequin's face. The flickering light made the shadows over its eyes jump. Hakeem gasped.

6. "What is it?" asked Malcolm.

"Watch," said Hakeem. They stood in front of the mannequin and waited. After a minute, the light overhead flickered.

"Whoa!" said Malcolm. "That looked like he was shifting his eyes!"

"That explains what Sammy saw," said Hakeem. "What about the noises?"

7. Malcolm started leaning from side to side and walked around the room like a duck. Each time he shifted his weight to one side, a floorboard creaked. As he wobbled around the room, the floorboards creaked and moaned.

Hakeem laughed. "This place is great!" he said. "I'm so glad my brother didn't scare me away!

10. Which of these is an example of personification from the story?

a. "There were just a few standing lamps and one small bulb on the ceiling to provide light."
b. "As he wobbled around the room, the floorboards creaked and moaned."
c. "Hakeem's third-grade class takes a field trip every spring to the county historical museum."
d. "We looked around to see if anyone else was there, but it was empty."

11. Which statement in paragraph 2 shows that Hakeem's mother does not trust Sammy?

a. "Gerard, stop scaring your brother."
b. "Hakeem, there is no such thing as ghosts."
c. "I'm sure there is a logical explanation to those noises."
d. "That's just Sammy's imagination getting out of hand."

12. What word best matches the description of Hakeem in paragraph three?

a. Honest
b. Happy
c. Brave
d. Angry

13. What word best matches the description of Gerard in paragraph three?

a. Happy
b. Honest
c. Angry
d. Brave

14. How does Hakeem change throughout the story?

a. Hakeem is first fearful but gains confidence.
b. Hakeem was very confident but became scared.
c. Hakeem was determined and then became lazy.
d. Hakeem is first slightly nervous but turns fearful.

15. What definition best matches the meaning of the word "dim" in paragraph five?

a. Badly lit
b. Dusty
c. Empty
d. Crowded

16. Why did Hakeem laugh in paragraph seven?

a. Malcolm walked like a duck in the old uniform room
b. The old uniform room was haunted
c. His brother, Gerard, lied to him about the old uniform room
d. He found out the old uniform room was not haunted

17. Which of the following statements tells the main idea of this story?

a. It is important to be brave.
b. Appearances can be deceiving.
c. Trust people older than you.
d. Historical museums are haunted.

18. What happened last in the story?

a. The county historian gives the class a tour.
b. The light flickered over the mannequin.
c. Malcolm starts walking like a duck.
d. Gerard told Hakeem about the haunted room in the museum.

Questions 19 -28 pertain to the following passage:

THE STATE FAIR OF TEXAS

Manuela wrote the following journal entry about her visit to the annual State Fair in Dallas, Texas.

October 11, 2009

My father woke me up early, at 6 a.m., so we could get to the Texas State Fair in time to get a good parking spot. This was my first visit to the fair. I am eight-years-old, and I live near Dallas, where the fair is held every year from late September to early October. We quickly ate breakfast. Dad put his coffee in a thermos cup so he could finish it on the drive.

It only took us 20 minutes to get to the fairgrounds, but we had to wait for 30 minutes to get a parking space! By the time we got into the fair, it was almost 8 a.m. We were at the fair to see my cousin Gloria with her prize goats. Gloria is four years older than I am. She lives on a farm near Austin where her family raises goats and sheep. They use the animals' milk to make cheese and the sheep's wool to make yarn. Gloria has five goats, and she was showing two of them.

Gloria's goats are Nubian. They have short hair and very long, dangly ears. Gloria's two goats are named Maja and Henry. Maja, a girl, is white with black and tan spots. Henry, a boy, is mostly black with white feet and a white spot on his throat.

Gloria was judged on how her goats looked and how they behaved in the ring. Gloria had washed and brushed both goats so they had very shiny coats. The goats were not very tall. Maja's head came up to my chest, and Henry was tall enough to rest his chin on my shoulder. Gloria said they were supposed to look well fed, but not fat.

"No ribs showing and no belly sticking out," she said as she walked Maja around the pen.

The goats also were judged on how well they behaved in front of the judges. Gloria got points if the goats followed her and did everything she told them to do. She lost points if the goats did not follow her or ran away. Gloria said that last year, her friend's goat got only halfway around the ring before a whistle scared him and he ran back to the gate.

Finally, it was time for Gloria to show her goats. She brought out Maja first. Maja was wearing a harness with a leash attached to it. Maja followed Gloria very quietly until they reached the judge's table. Then Maja began to bleat. At first, she bleated softly, but then she got louder. By the time Gloria brought her back to the gate, Maja was bleating very loudly.

I wondered if the judges took away points if the goat was noisy while it was being shown. Henry was much better. He did everything Gloria told him to do without making a sound. I thought for sure Henry would get a prize.

After Gloria was finished, we waited for the judges to announce the prizes. We were so surprised when Maja got second place!

"I guess the judges understand goat," joked Gloria, as she showed off her prizes. Henry only got an honorable mention.

We had a great time at the fair. I learned a lesson from Maja. The squeaky wheel gets the grease after all!

19. Which name goes into the box at the top of the diagram?

a. Maja
b. Gloria
c. Henry
d. Manuela

20. What is the best summary of this journal entry?

a. Manuela recounts her visit to the Texas State Fair to watch her cousin Gloria show her goats.
b. Manuela recounts her visit to the Texas State Fair where she got to show her goats.
c. Manuela recounts her visit to the Texas State Fair and riding rides.
d. Manuela recounts her visits to the Texas State Fair and winning a stuffed animal from one of the carnival games.

21. What is the main idea of this journal entry?

a. Being brave can lead to great opportunities.
b. Being small doesn't make you less capable.
c. Being determined will help you achieve your dreams.
d. Being unique can lead to success.

22. How does Manuela change throughout the story?

a. Manuela thought showing goats was silly at first, but then she grew to like it.
b. Manuela first thought there was only one way to reach success, but she gained a new perspective and realized there are many ways to reach success.
c. Manuela didn't want her cousin's goats to win, but then she was excited when Maja got second place.
d. Manuela wanted to go on rides at the fair, but she ended up enjoying the rodeo instead.

23. Which other character in Manuela's story changes some?

a. Her dad
b. Maja
c. Gloria
d. Henry

24. The chart shows the order of some events from the story.

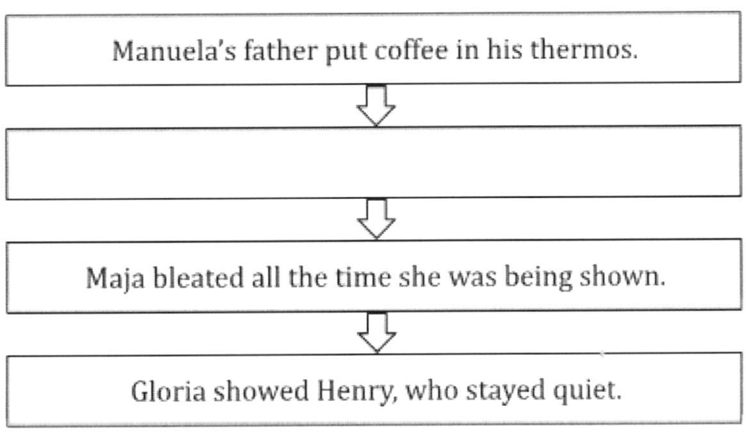

Which event belongs in the empty box?

a. Manuela had a great time at the fair
b. Manuela got up at 6 a.m.
c. Manuela and her father waited half-an-hour to park
d. Gloria won two prizes for her goats

25. Manuela woke up at 6 a.m. for the fair. How many hours later was it before she got into the fair?

a. Two
b. Three
c. Two and a half
d. One and a half

26. Which of these sentences from the entry is a metaphor?

a. "Finally, it was time for Gloria to show her goats."
b. "The squeaky wheel gets the grease after all!"
c. "I wondered if the judges took away points if the goat was noisy while it was being shown."
d. "Gloria had washed and brushed both goats so they had very shiny coats."

27. Why do you think the judges picked Maja instead of Henry?

a. Maja was better groomed than Henry.
b. Maja's loud behavior stood out and was more rememberable.
c. Maja was sweeter than Henry.
d. Maja performed the task of following Gloria better than Henry did.

28. What does "the squeaky wheel gets the grease" mean in this story?

a. Manuela had a great day at the fair
b. Henry got an award for being quiet
c. Gloria won two prizes for her goats
d. Maja was noisy, but she still won a prize

Questions 29 – 34 pertain to the following invitation:

Patricio's Party

29. What type of text is this?

a. Narrative
b. Informational
c. Poetry
d. Argumentative

30. What is the purpose of this text?

a. To invite people to a slumber party
b. To announce the arrival of a new baby
c. To invite people to a birthday party
d. To announce Patricio is another year older

31. How does the author want a response?

a. Phone call or text message
b. Email
c. In person
d. By mail

32. Why do you think the author wants a response to the invitation?

a. The author needs to know if they will all fit in the pool.
b. The author needs to know how much food to make.
c. The author needs to know what types of games to plan.
d. The author needs to know how many horses to reserve.

33. What type of party is this invitation for?

a. House warming
b. Anniversary
c. Graduation
d. Birthday

34. What is the main activity at the party?

a. Playing games
b. Eating cake
c. Swimming
d. Horseback riding

Questions 35 – 40 pertain to the following passage:

When I Am Sick

At least once a year my nose gets red,
and I cough and sniffle and sneeze.
My mother tucks me into bed
with a heavy blanket, so I won't freeze.
She feeds me a teaspoon of medicine,
it is purple and very thick.
It tastes like grapes and drips on my chin,
but it makes me feel better quick.
My mother stays home from work,
she reads me books and lets me watch TV.
I do not like feeling sick,
but I love having my mother all to me.

35. What type of poem is this?

a. Free verse
b. Rhymed verse
c. Haiku
d. Limerick

36. What does the mother do when the author is sick?

a. Takes her temperature
b. Tucks her into bed
c. Calls the doctor
d. Makes tea

37. What is the best summary of the poem?

a. A child finds comfort in the loving care of their mother while sick.
b. A mother finds comfort in the loving care of their child while sick.
c. A child fakes being sick to receive special care from their mother.
d. A mother fakes being sick to receive special care from their child.

38. What best describes the author's perspective of being sick?

a. The author loves being sick because her mom takes such good care of her.
b. The author loves being sick, but she does not like the way her mom takes care of her when she is sick.
c. The author does not like being sick because her mom doesn't take care of her at all.
d. The author does not like being sick, but she values the way her mom cares for her while sick.

39. Which of these phrases from the poem displays a hyperbole?

a. "so I won't freeze"
b. "it is purple and very thick"
c. "I cough and sniffle and sneeze"
d. "my nose gets red"

40. Which of the following does the author's mother not do?

a. Reads books
b. Gives medicine
c. Makes soup
d. Tucks her in bed

How to Overcome Test Anxiety

Just the thought of taking a test is enough to make most people a little nervous. A test is an important event that can have a long-term impact on your future, so it's important to take it seriously and it's natural to feel anxious about performing well. But just because anxiety is normal, that doesn't mean that it's helpful in test taking, or that you should simply accept it as part of your life. Anxiety can have a variety of effects. These effects can be mild, like making you feel slightly nervous, or severe, like blocking your ability to focus or remember even a simple detail.

If you experience test anxiety—whether severe or mild—it's important to know how to beat it. To discover this, first you need to understand what causes test anxiety.

Causes of Test Anxiety

While we often think of anxiety as an uncontrollable emotional state, it can actually be caused by simple, practical things. One of the most common causes of test anxiety is that a person does not feel adequately prepared for their test. This feeling can be the result of many different issues such as poor study habits or lack of organization, but the most common culprit is time management. Starting to study too late, failing to organize your study time to cover all of the material, or being distracted while you study will mean that you're not well prepared for the test. This may lead to cramming the night before, which will cause you to be physically and mentally exhausted for the test. Poor time management also contributes to feelings of stress, fear, and hopelessness as you realize you are not well prepared but don't know what to do about it.

Other times, test anxiety is not related to your preparation for the test but comes from unresolved fear. This may be a past failure on a test, or poor performance on tests in general. It may come from comparing yourself to others who seem to be performing better or from the stress of living up to expectations. Anxiety may be driven by fears of the future—how failure on this test would affect your educational and career goals. These fears are often completely irrational, but they can still negatively impact your test performance.

Elements of Test Anxiety

As mentioned earlier, test anxiety is considered to be an emotional state, but it has physical and mental components as well. Sometimes you may not even realize that you are suffering from test anxiety until you notice the physical symptoms. These can include trembling hands, rapid heartbeat, sweating, nausea, and tense muscles. Extreme anxiety may lead to fainting or vomiting. Obviously, any of these symptoms can have a negative impact on testing. It is important to recognize them as soon as they begin to occur so that you can address the problem before it damages your performance.

The mental components of test anxiety include trouble focusing and inability to remember learned information. During a test, your mind is on high alert, which can help you recall information and stay focused for an extended period of time. However, anxiety interferes with your mind's natural processes, causing you to blank out, even on the questions you know well. The strain of testing during anxiety makes it difficult to stay focused, especially on a test that may take several hours. Extreme anxiety can take a huge mental toll, making it difficult not only to recall test information but even to understand the test questions or pull your thoughts together.

Effects of Test Anxiety

Test anxiety is like a disease—if left untreated, it will get progressively worse. Anxiety leads to poor performance, and this reinforces the feelings of fear and failure, which in turn lead to poor performances on subsequent tests. It can grow from a mild nervousness to a crippling condition. If allowed to progress, test anxiety can have a big impact on your schooling, and consequently on your future.

Test anxiety can spread to other parts of your life. Anxiety on tests can become anxiety in any stressful situation, and blanking on a test can turn into panicking in a job situation. But fortunately, you don't have to let anxiety rule your testing and determine your grades. There are a number of relatively simple steps you can take to move past anxiety and function normally on a test and in the rest of life.

Physical Steps for Beating Test Anxiety

While test anxiety is a serious problem, the good news is that it can be overcome. It doesn't have to control your ability to think and remember information. While it may take time, you can begin taking steps today to beat anxiety.

Just as your first hint that you may be struggling with anxiety comes from the physical symptoms, the first step to treating it is also physical. Rest is crucial for having a clear, strong mind. If you are tired, it is much easier to give in to anxiety. But if you establish good sleep habits, your body and mind will be ready to perform optimally, without the strain of exhaustion. Additionally, sleeping well helps you to retain information better, so you're more likely to recall the answers when you see the test questions.

Getting good sleep means more than going to bed on time. It's important to allow your brain time to relax. Take study breaks from time to time so it doesn't get overworked, and don't study right before bed. Take time to rest your mind before trying to rest your body, or you may find it difficult to fall asleep.

Along with sleep, other aspects of physical health are important in preparing for a test. Good nutrition is vital for good brain function. Sugary foods and drinks may give a burst of energy but this burst is followed by a crash, both physically and emotionally. Instead, fuel your body with protein and vitamin-rich foods.

Also, drink plenty of water. Dehydration can lead to headaches and exhaustion, especially if your brain is already under stress from the rigors of the test. Particularly if your test is a long one, drink water during the breaks. And if possible, take an energy-boosting snack to eat between sections.

Along with sleep and diet, a third important part of physical health is exercise. Maintaining a steady workout schedule is helpful, but even taking 5-minute study breaks to walk can help get your blood pumping faster and clear your head. Exercise also releases endorphins, which contribute to a positive feeling and can help combat test anxiety.

When you nurture your physical health, you are also contributing to your mental health. If your body is healthy, your mind is much more likely to be healthy as well. So take time to rest, nourish your body with healthy food and water, and get moving as much as possible. Taking these physical steps will make you stronger and more able to take the mental steps necessary to overcome test anxiety.

Mental Steps for Beating Test Anxiety

Working on the mental side of test anxiety can be more challenging, but as with the physical side, there are clear steps you can take to overcome it. As mentioned earlier, test anxiety often stems from lack of preparation, so the obvious solution is to prepare for the test. Effective studying may be the most important weapon you have for beating test anxiety, but you can and should employ several other mental tools to combat fear.

First, boost your confidence by reminding yourself of past success—tests or projects that you aced. If you're putting as much effort into preparing for this test as you did for those, there's no reason you should expect to fail here. Work hard to prepare; then trust your preparation.

Second, surround yourself with encouraging people. It can be helpful to find a study group, but be sure that the people you're around will encourage a positive attitude. If you spend time with others who are anxious or cynical, this will only contribute to your own anxiety. Look for others who are motivated to study hard from a desire to succeed, not from a fear of failure.

Third, reward yourself. A test is physically and mentally tiring, even without anxiety, and it can be helpful to have something to look forward to. Plan an activity following the test, regardless of the outcome, such as going to a movie or getting ice cream.

When you are taking the test, if you find yourself beginning to feel anxious, remind yourself that you know the material. Visualize successfully completing the test. Then take a few deep, relaxing breaths and return to it. Work through the questions carefully but with confidence, knowing that you are capable of succeeding.

Developing a healthy mental approach to test taking will also aid in other areas of life. Test anxiety affects more than just the actual test—it can be damaging to your mental health and even contribute to depression. It's important to beat test anxiety before it becomes a problem for more than testing.

Study Strategy

Being prepared for the test is necessary to combat anxiety, but what does being prepared look like? You may study for hours on end and still not feel prepared. What you need is a strategy for test prep. The next few pages outline our recommended steps to help you plan out and conquer the challenge of preparation.

Step 1: Scope Out the Test

Learn everything you can about the format (multiple choice, essay, etc.) and what will be on the test. Gather any study materials, course outlines, or sample exams that may be available. Not only will this help you to prepare, but knowing what to expect can help to alleviate test anxiety.

Step 2: Map Out the Material

Look through the textbook or study guide and make note of how many chapters or sections it has. Then divide these over the time you have. For example, if a book has 15 chapters and you have five days to study, you need to cover three chapters each day. Even better, if you have the time, leave an extra day at the end for overall review after you have gone through the material in depth.

If time is limited, you may need to prioritize the material. Look through it and make note of which sections you think you already have a good grasp on, and which need review. While you are studying, skim quickly through the familiar sections and take more time on the challenging parts.

Write out your plan so you don't get lost as you go. Having a written plan also helps you feel more in control of the study, so anxiety is less likely to arise from feeling overwhelmed at the amount to cover.

Step 3: Gather Your Tools

Decide what study method works best for you. Do you prefer to highlight in the book as you study and then go back over the highlighted portions? Or do you type out notes of the important information? Or is it helpful to make flashcards that you can carry with you? Assemble the pens, index cards, highlighters, post-it notes, and any other materials you may need so you won't be distracted by getting up to find things while you study.

If you're having a hard time retaining the information or organizing your notes, experiment with different methods. For example, try color-coding by subject with colored pens, highlighters, or post-it notes. If you learn better by hearing, try recording yourself reading your notes so you can listen while in the car, working out, or simply sitting at your desk. Ask a friend to quiz you from your flashcards, or try teaching someone the material to solidify it in your mind.

Step 4: Create Your Environment

It's important to avoid distractions while you study. This includes both the obvious distractions like visitors and the subtle distractions like an uncomfortable chair (or a too-comfortable couch that makes you want to fall asleep). Set up the best study environment possible: good lighting and a comfortable work area. If background music helps you focus, you may want to turn it on, but otherwise keep the room quiet. If you are using a computer to take notes, be sure you don't have any other windows open, especially applications like social media, games, or anything else that could distract you. Silence your phone and turn off notifications. Be sure to keep water close by so you stay hydrated while you study (but avoid unhealthy drinks and snacks).

Also, take into account the best time of day to study. Are you freshest first thing in the morning? Try to set aside some time then to work through the material. Is your mind clearer in the afternoon or evening? Schedule your study session then. Another method is to study at the same time of day that you will take the test, so that your brain gets used to working on the material at that time and will be ready to focus at test time.

Step 5: Study!

Once you have done all the study preparation, it's time to settle into the actual studying. Sit down, take a few moments to settle your mind so you can focus, and begin to follow your study plan. Don't give in to distractions or let yourself procrastinate. This is your time to prepare so you'll be ready to fearlessly approach the test. Make the most of the time and stay focused.

Of course, you don't want to burn out. If you study too long you may find that you're not retaining the information very well. Take regular study breaks. For example, taking five minutes out of every hour to walk briskly, breathing deeply and swinging your arms, can help your mind stay fresh.

As you get to the end of each chapter or section, it's a good idea to do a quick review. Remind yourself of what you learned and work on any difficult parts. When you feel that you've mastered the material, move on to the next part. At the end of your study session, briefly skim through your notes again.

But while review is helpful, cramming last minute is NOT. If at all possible, work ahead so that you won't need to fit all your study into the last day. Cramming overloads your brain with more information than it can process and retain, and your tired mind may struggle to recall even previously learned information when it is overwhelmed with last-minute study. Also, the urgent nature of cramming and the stress placed on your brain contribute to anxiety. You'll be more likely to go to the test feeling unprepared and having trouble thinking clearly.

So don't cram, and don't stay up late before the test, even just to review your notes at a leisurely pace. Your brain needs rest more than it needs to go over the information again. In fact, plan to finish your studies by noon or early afternoon the day before the test. Give your brain the rest of the day to relax or focus on other things, and get a good night's sleep. Then you will be fresh for the test and better able to recall what you've studied.

Step 6: Take a Practice Test

Many courses offer sample tests, either online or in the study materials. This is an excellent resource to check whether you have mastered the material, as well as to prepare for the test format and environment.

Check the test format ahead of time: the number of questions, the type (multiple choice, free response, etc.), and the time limit. Then create a plan for working through them. For example, if you have 30 minutes to take a 60-question test, your limit is 30 seconds per question. Spend less time on the questions you know well so that you can take more time on the difficult ones.

If you have time to take several practice tests, take the first one open book, with no time limit. Work through the questions at your own pace and make sure you fully understand them. Gradually work up to taking a test under test conditions: sit at a desk with all study materials put away and set a timer. Pace yourself to make sure you finish the test with time to spare and go back to check your answers if you have time.

After each test, check your answers. On the questions you missed, be sure you understand why you missed them. Did you misread the question (tests can use tricky wording)? Did you forget the information? Or was it something you hadn't learned? Go back and study any shaky areas that the practice tests reveal.

Taking these tests not only helps with your grade, but also aids in combating test anxiety. If you're already used to the test conditions, you're less likely to worry about it, and working through tests until you're scoring well gives you a confidence boost. Go through the practice tests until you feel comfortable, and then you can go into the test knowing that you're ready for it.

Test Tips

On test day, you should be confident, knowing that you've prepared well and are ready to answer the questions. But aside from preparation, there are several test day strategies you can employ to maximize your performance.

First, as stated before, get a good night's sleep the night before the test (and for several nights before that, if possible). Go into the test with a fresh, alert mind rather than staying up late to study.

Try not to change too much about your normal routine on the day of the test. It's important to eat a nutritious breakfast, but if you normally don't eat breakfast at all, consider eating just a protein bar. If you're a coffee drinker, go ahead and have your normal coffee. Just make sure you time it so that the caffeine doesn't wear off right in the middle of your test. Avoid sugary beverages, and drink enough water to stay hydrated but not so much that you need a restroom break 10 minutes into the test. If your test isn't first thing in the morning, consider going for a walk or doing a light workout before the test to get your blood flowing.

Allow yourself enough time to get ready, and leave for the test with plenty of time to spare so you won't have the anxiety of scrambling to arrive in time. Another reason to be early is to select a good seat. It's helpful to sit away from doors and windows, which can be distracting. Find a good seat, get out your supplies, and settle your mind before the test begins.

When the test begins, start by going over the instructions carefully, even if you already know what to expect. Make sure you avoid any careless mistakes by following the directions.

Then begin working through the questions, pacing yourself as you've practiced. If you're not sure on an answer, don't spend too much time on it, and don't let it shake your confidence. Either skip it and come back later, or eliminate as many wrong answers as possible and guess among the remaining ones. Don't dwell on these questions as you continue—put them out of your mind and focus on what lies ahead.

Be sure to read all of the answer choices, even if you're sure the first one is the right answer. Sometimes you'll find a better one if you keep reading. But don't second-guess yourself if you do immediately know the answer. Your gut instinct is usually right. Don't let test anxiety rob you of the information you know.

If you have time at the end of the test (and if the test format allows), go back and review your answers. Be cautious about changing any, since your first instinct tends to be correct, but make sure you didn't misread any of the questions or accidentally mark the wrong answer choice. Look over any you skipped and make an educated guess.

At the end, leave the test feeling confident. You've done your best, so don't waste time worrying about your performance or wishing you could change anything. Instead, celebrate the successful completion of this test. And finally, use this test to learn how to deal with anxiety even better next time.

Review Video: Test Anxiety
Visit mometrix.com/academy and enter code: 100340

Important Qualification

Not all anxiety is created equal. If your test anxiety is causing major issues in your life beyond the classroom or testing center, or if you are experiencing troubling physical symptoms related to your anxiety, it may be a sign of a serious physiological or psychological condition. If this sounds like your situation, we strongly encourage you to seek professional help.

Online Resources

Due to our efforts to try to keep this book to a manageable length, we've created a link that will give you access to all of your online resources:

mometrix.com/resources719/flg3elarwb

It's Your Moment, Let's Celebrate It!

Share your story @mometrixtestpreparation

Mometrix
TEST PREPARATION

Florida

Grade 3 ELA Reading Test Prep Workbook Answer Key

DEAR FUTURE EXAM SUCCESS STORY

First of all, **THANK YOU** for purchasing Mometrix study materials!

Second, congratulations! You are one of the few determined test-takers who are committed to doing whatever it takes to excel on your exam. **You have come to the right place.** We developed these study materials with one goal in mind: to deliver you the information you need in a format that's concise and easy to use.

In addition to optimizing your guide for the content of the test, we've outlined our recommended steps for breaking down the preparation process into small, attainable goals so you can make sure you stay on track.

We've also analyzed the entire test-taking process, identifying the most common pitfalls and showing how you can overcome them and be ready for any curveball the test throws you.

Standardized testing is one of the biggest obstacles on your road to success, which only increases the importance of doing well in the high-pressure, high-stakes environment of test day. Your results on this test could have a significant impact on your future, and this guide provides the information and practical advice to help you achieve your full potential on test day.

Your success is our success

We would love to hear from you! If you would like to share the story of your exam success or if you have any questions or comments in regard to our products, please contact us at **800-673-8175** or **support@mometrix.com**.

Thanks again for your business and we wish you continued success!

Sincerely,
The Mometrix Test Preparation Team

Written and edited by the Mometrix Exam Secrets Test Prep Team
Printed in the United States of America

Table of Contents

Workbook Answers

Reading Prose and Poetry

How Nian Was Defeated

1. ocean

2. shaking or trembling

3. great fear, terror

4. Even though the story isn't true, it still has a central lesson or point. The central lesson of the story is how the customs of Chinese New Year's celebrations came about.

5. C: This story is a myth and so is *The Legend of Paul Bunyan*, while all the other books contain true stories.

Poems

1. A: *A Jelly Fish* is a free verse poem. free verse poems do not follow a specific rhyme scheme or meter. There is no regular pattern.

2. D: *There Was A Small Boy Of Quebec* is a limerick poem. Limericks consist of five lines. The rhyme scheme of a limerick poem is AABBA, and they are also typically somewhat humorous.

3. C: *Old Pond* is a haiku poem. Haiku poems are traditional Japanese poems that consist of three lines with a 5-7-5 syllable pattern. Typically, they capture moments of nature.

4. B: *Bed in Summer* is a rhymed verse poem. It follows the rhyme scheme of AABB.

5. C: Each poem exhibits some form of simplicity. *A Jelly Fish* doesn't rely on complex language, and it uses clear imagery to describe the jellyfish's beauty. *There Was A Small Boy Of Quebec* uses simple phrasing to make the poem easy to understand and read. *Old Pond* uses few words to capture a specific moment of nature. *Bed in Summer* uses simple, child-like language to convey a simple theme rather than complex emotions.

Reading Informational Texts

Our Neighbor Mercury

1. Mercury is the tiny planet closest to the sun.

2. D

3. craters

4. According to the text, "the [planet] that is closest to the sun is named Mercury." Therefore, it is safe to assume that Mercury is so much hotter than Earther due to its distance from the Sun compared to Earth's distance from the sun.

Montana: Big Sky Country

1. A

2. B

3. D

4. D

Linda Richards, Medical Pioneer

1. C

2. B

3. The correct order from top to bottom is 4, 1, 3. 2

Reading Across Genres & Vocabulary

The Big Picture

Mom's Big Idea

1. Janey's mom says cars and trucks are "flying down the road." She means they are going at high rates of speed.

2. C

3. B

4. "Don't keep us in the dark" is the figurative phrase. He means that Janey's mom shouldn't keep her idea a secret from them.

5. D

Mom Makes a List

1. C

2. A

3. She uses the phrase "all your ducks in a row", which means to be organized and ready to go

4. mil | lion do | main tech | nic | al host | ing

5. B

Mom Launches Her Website

1. It means she couldn't figure out exactly what was different. People use this expression when they know something is wrong, or different, but don't know exactly what is wrong or different.

2. D

3. A "night owl" is someone who likes to stay up very, very late.

4. C

5. A

Lights! Camera! Janey!

1. C

2. B

3. D

4. A

5. C

A Team Effort

1. C

2. activity congratulate

3. D

4. She means it's something she enjoys a lot.

5. congratulate

Polar Bears

1. B

2. To accomplish a goal; to achieve what one sets out to do

3. C

4. B

Walrus

1. *get older*

2. An animal that kills and eats another animal

3. A

4. D

Levi Coffin: President of the Underground Railroad

1. d

2. Fugitive

3. illegal

4. legal and -il

5. The correct order from top to bottom is 2, 4, 1, 3.

One Giant Leap for Mankind

1. Because no one had ever done it before (or) Because it had seemed impossible for centuries

2. brave

3. C

4. B

Phonics, Language, Grammar, and Word Recognition

Prefixes

1. D

2. C

3. A

4. B

5. C

6. C

7. A

8. B

9. B

10. D

11. A

12. B

13. D

14. C

15. A

Suffixes

1. D

2. A

3. C

4. C

5. B

6. D

7. A

8. C

9. B

10. D

Understanding Latin Suffixes

1. kings, queens, princes and princesses = royalty

2. money given to someone for doing something = payment

3. scare the daylights out of = terrify

4. having nothing to eat for a long time = starvation

5. lights and appliances are powered by this = electricity

6. a big party = celebration

7. able to be bent = bendable

8. swear to tell the truth = testify

9. worthy of being looked up to = admirable

10. able to be divided = divisible

Multisyllable Words

1. bowl/ing

2. play/ground

3. bas/ket/ball

4. soc/cer

5. ref/er/ee

6. gym/nast

7.goal/post

8. catch/er

9. out/field/er

10. base/ball

11. quar/ter/back

12. o/ver/time

13. vol/ley/ball

14. um/pire

15. win/ner

16. tack/le

17. score/board

18. fum/ble

19. strike/out

20. ho/mer

Spelling Irregular Words

1. C: friend

2. C: mother

3. C: would

4. A: humor

5. D: busy

6. D: height

7. A: weight

8. B: straight

9. B: Wednesday

10. B: been

11. C: kind

12. A: tissue

13. D: women

14. B: sugar

15. D: laugh

16. D: doubt

17. B: bought

18. A: business

19. D: lose

20. A: could

Parts of Speech

1. adjectives

2. nouns

3. verbs

4. adverbs

5. pronouns

Plural Nouns

1. tornadoes

2. feet

3. fish

4. elves

5. tomatoes

6. men

7. calves

8. wives

9. towns

10. mice

Concrete Versus Abstract Nouns

1. A

2. C

3. C

4. A

5. A

6. C

7. A

8. C

9. C

10. A

Regular and Irregular Verbs

1. bought
2. kept
3. hung
4. knew
5. met
6. put
7. went
8. lost
9. brought
10. drank

Simple Verb Tenses

1. will taste
2. ran
3. will have
4. will kick
5. talk
6. flew
7. slept
8. will speak
9. wake
10. thought

Subject/Verb Agreement Part 1

1. teach
2. knows
3. meows
4. sings
5. gallop
6. drink

7. ring

8. hold

9. reads

10. cuts

SUBJECT/VERB AGREEMENT PART 2

1. imagine – R

2. are – W (is)

3. drive – R

4. travels – R

5. Think – R

6. takes – W (take)

7. goes – W (go)

8. does –W (do)

9. depend – W (depends)

10. makes – W (make)

PRONOUN/ANTECEDENT AGREEMENT PART 1

1. my

2. their

3. her

4. my

5. us

6. mine

7. her

8. his

9. its

10. they

PRONOUN/ANTECEDENT AGREEMENT PART 2

1. Gabrielle she

2. belongs to him his

3. Uncle Bob and Aunt Sally they

4. Fred he

5. belongs to you and me ours

6. belongs to me my

7. you and me us

8. belongs to the team theirs

9. belongs to her hers

10. the toy it

Adjectives

1. messier

2. friendliest

3. tallest

4. worst

5. heavier

6. more athletic

7. saddest

8. longer

9. roughest

10. bigger

Adverbs

1. most quickly

2. more loudly (or louder)

3. better

4. more promptly

5. harder

6. slower (or more slowly)

7. most rapidly

8. earlier

9. soonest

10. more neatly

Compound Versus Complex Sentences

1. compound

2. complex

3. complex

4. compound

5. complex

6. complex

7. complex

8. compound

9. compound

10. complex

Compound Sentences

1. Fred has the flu, and Carol has a cold.

2. I like baseball, but I don't like basketball.

3. You can eat lunch now, or you can eat lunch later.

4. You should study hard, so you can pass your test.

5. We read about art museums, and our teacher told us about famous painters.

Complex Sentences

For each problem, either of the answers shown is correct.

1. When the bell rings, it's time for lunch. | It's time for lunch when the bell rings.

2. If you're not feeling well, you should stay home. | You should stay home if you're not feeling well.

3. Unless you eat your vegetables, you won't get dessert. | You won't get dessert unless you eat your vegetables.

4. You must clean your room before you may go outside and play. | Before you may go outside and play, you must clean your room.

5. Watch out for traffic while you ride your bike. | While you ride your bike, watch out for traffic.

Capitalization in Titles

1. Why You Should Exercise Daily

2. Now They Tell Me!

3. North to Alaska

4. The Hound of the Baskervilles

5. A Tale of Two Cities

6. Please Don't Eat the Daisies

7. Indiana Jones and the Last Crusade

8. Uncle Tom's Cabin

9. The Night Before Christmas

10. Willy Wonka and the Chocolate Factory

Commas and Quotation Marks

1. Boise, Idaho

2. "Mom doesn't want us to have snacks before supper," Billy reminded Joanie.

3. Frieda asked, "What time does the bus usually get here?"

4. "Sir," Pedro exclaimed, "you dropped your wallet!" (Or "Sir," Pedro exclaimed, "you dropped your wallet.")

5. Paris, France

6. "Are those your sunglasses?" Molly asked

7. "James and Kirk," said Mr. Brown, "you need to see me after class."

8. Des Moines, Iowa

9. Dad said, "Let's go to the beach this Saturday."

10. "I don't think that's a very good idea, Mabel," her mother replied.

Possessives

1. Let's say hello to Tanequa's mom.

2. This is Jack's uniform.

3. I rode Freddy's new bike.

4. Here's the baby's bib.

5. The horse's stall needs cleaned.

6. Here's your book.

7. This is Charles's new video game.

8. Your bus is coming.

9. The dog wagged its tail.

10. The boys' fingers were freezing after they built the snowman.

High Frequency Words

1. impossible

2. probably

3. everybody

4. weather

5. beautiful

6. prettiest

7. laughed

8. question

9. because

10. discover

Base Words and Suffixes

1. scary

2. exciting

3. interesting

4. replacement

5. newest

6. hopeless

7. muddy

8. accidental

9. happiness

10. musicians

Word and Phrase Choice

1. C

2. A

3. B

4. C

5. B

6. C

7. B

8. C

9. A

10. A

Spoken and Written English

1. S

2. W

3. W

4. S

5. S

6. S

7. W

8. W

9. S

10. W

Root Words

1. C

2. B

3. A

4. C

5. C

6. A

7. B

8. A

9. B

10. C

Suffix and Prefix Additions

1. disagree

2. unbelievable

3. happiness

4. redo

5. impolite

6. quickly

7. awareness

8. teacher

9. magical

10. cautious

Figurative Language

1. Personification

2. Simile

3.Simile

4. Hyperbole

5. Personification

6. Hyperbole

7. Metaphor

8. Personification

9. Metaphor

10. Hyperbole

Answers and Explanations for Test #1

1. C: The first paragraph mostly describes Miguel's behavior and actions as a five-year-old during walks with his father. "...he liked to pick up branches and hit them against the ground and the trees. Sometimes he would waive the stick and pretend he was fighting a great battle."

2. D: Miguel showed more interest in the woods by asking his father questions about different trees and plants. As a result of his interest, Miguel learned how to identify trees by their bark and leaves and how trees reproduce by spreading their seeds to other parts of the forest.

3. C: In this paragraph, the word identify is used to show the action of recognizing, or identifying by sight, different trees and plants by the appearance of their bark or leaves. It is different from understanding well because Miguel doesn't have to understand trees very well to identify their leaves and bark.

4. B: The central theme of this story is empathy. This is shown through Miguel's development of his sense of responsibility in caring for the environment. The act of wanting to put the leaves back how they originally were displayed this empathy and growth since he was worried that by messing the leaves up, the ants would not have a place to hide. The story does not exhibit any selfish behavior, heroism, or independence.

5. A: The theme shifts from ignorance in the beginning of the story to empathy towards the end of the story. At first, Miguel is depicted as a young child who does not yet appreciate or value the natural world around him. By the end of the story, Miguel has shown growth and wants to help protect the world and other living creatures around him.

6. D: Throughout the story, Mr. Gonzalez's character slightly shifts. In the beginning, he acted as more of a teacher to Miguel. He patiently instructed Miguel about the natural world and things they encountered on their walk. Later in the story, he became more of an observer as he watched Miguel interact with nature, and he recognized Miguel's growth.

7. A: On Miguel's journey in nature, he ended up recognizing the need to take responsibility for his actions. He at first was exhibiting childish behaviors, but then he realized that his actions have consequences. Thus, he wanted to rectify what he had done by fixing the leaves for the ants. This represents maturing.

8. A: In the story, Miguel's father tells him not to kick the log after we learned that he used to play with sticks when he was younger and before Miguel and his father leave the log and Miguel returns to replace the bark and leaves they brushed aside.

9. B: Miguel's father points out how Miguel's attitude toward the log changes. Usually, people love things that they want to protect. Hating something is usually the opposite of wanting to protect it.

10. C: Miguel's change in attitude towards nature reflects the golden rule since at first Miguel did not care about the creatures living in the log. He was only concerned about how it affected him. However, when Miguel returned to make sure the leaves were put back to ensure the ants had a place to hide if needed, his attitude shifted. He started to treat the creatures the way he would like to be treated.

11. B: Mr. Gonzalez encourages independent thinking and self-reflection through accountability. He does this by stopping Miguel and asking how he would feel if a giant kicked their house. This conversation encourages Miguel to think for himself and reflect on how his actions affect others. While Miguel does end up attempting to fix the leaves from his mistake, Mr. Gonzalez does not instruct or guide him to do so. Mr. Gonzalez also does not get mad at Miguel for his selfish behaviors, but, rather, he wants to draw attention to Miguel's selfish behaviors in order to help Miguel learn.

12. C: Based on the answer of "it moved so fast" in Part A, it can be assumed that "dart" means a quick movement.

13. A: A hyperbole is an exaggerated statement that is not meant to be taken literally. While Maize is a good friend for Tanya to have, it is unlikely that she is the best friend a girl could have since she is a dog. Tanya was simply stating that she is a really good friend.

14. D: Tanya promised her mother that she would take care of Maize. As part of that promise, Tanya had to be home every day to help feed and take care of her dog. Tanya could not go over to her friends' houses after school. After a while Tanya began to miss seeing her friends outside of school.

15. A: Laticia helped solve Tanya's problem by inviting herself over to Tanya's house. This way, Tanya could see her friends and take care of her dog at the same time.

16. B: The best summary of this story is that Tanya finds a puppy in the grocery parking lot, and, regardless of initial challenges, she grows to love the puppy as her new friend and companion.

17. C: Tanya was very overwhelmed at first while trying to care for the dog, but she eventually grew to love and value the relationship she had developed with the dog. There was a point when she wished she had never gotten the dog in the first place, but that quickly changed.

18. C: The central idea of this passage is that bats are beneficial to people; however, bats are commonly misunderstood. Many people are scared of them because they associate them with sharp teeth, nighttime activity, and the idea that they might bite humans.

19. B: The only piece of text evidence that does not support the central idea is that all bats are mammals. This is a fact about bats, but it does not play a role in supporting the central idea.

20. A: The author's purpose of this text is to inform and clear up any misconceptions people have about bats.

21. A: To best support the claim that bats help the ecosystem, the author can talk about how most bats eat insects. The author could then further elaborate how insects can harm plants, and if the plants die, other organisms will also be affected. Therefore, bats act as a natural pesticide, and they help the ecosystem maintain a balance.

22. D: The space in the middle of a Venn diagram lists the components that the two sides of the diagram have in common. Both kinds of bats only come out at night.

23. D: A disease is an illness or sickness. It is not an injury. It also is not abnormal growth changes in the body that happen during fetal development, and it is not an immune overreaction by the body to a substance.

24. C: The title states that bats are our friends, so it can be inferred that bats are helpful and not harmful to humans. Just because they are our friends does not mean we should make them pets. Bats can also not understand our feelings, and it is unlikely that they will bring humans happiness.

25. C: This choice best summarizes the main idea of the poem, which is about a child at first adoring a toy, but eventually outgrowing it. Like lots of children, she stopped playing with the toy, but kept it for the memories and out of affection for the toy.

26. B: This poem is best classified as rhymed verse since it has a consistent rhyme scheme in each stanza. Bear and everywhere rhyme. Pool and cool rhyme. Looks and crooks rhyme. Shelf and elf rhyme. Away and stay rhyme.

27. A: The theme of this poem is reflecting on "the good old days". This simply means that the author is reflecting back to childhood and had a teddy bear named Sam. The poem is not about solving conflict, experiencing romantic love, or depicting an identity crisis.

28. D: While the narrator still cherished Sam deeply, the narrator outgrew the need to carry Sam around everywhere. The narrator grew and matured.

29. A: The narrator still values Sam deeply, but since he has grown up, he no longer idolizes him. He doesn't feel like he needs to take Sam everywhere he goes. The narrator acknowledges that he is too old for Sam, but he also still treasures him.

30. C: The word "crooks" in the poem means shape or curve. The sentence is "His fur wore off in patches and his ears bent into crooks."

31. A: The correct order of events in this poem is: Child receives Sam. Child takes Sam everywhere. Child puts Sam on a shelf.

32. A: The main idea of the passage is simply that Jake learned about the essential components of making a fire. While he did get to spend quality time with his dad and make dinner, those are not the main idea of the entire passage.

33. A: By wrapping his finger and thumb in a circle shape around the branches, Jake illustrated the concept of circumference, which is the measure around a circle.

34. B: The theme of this passage is learning and discovery. Jake learns and discovers how to make a fire and other facts about fire.

35. D: Jake make subtle changes throughout the passage as he becomes more knowledgeable about fire. He does not lose his curiosity about the fire, and he does not become arrogant about his skills. He also does not decide he wants to become a fireman when he grows up.

36. D: In the story Jake gets wood first, then his father starts the fire, and finally Jake gets out hot dogs to cook on the fire.

37. C: Jake's perspective lacks experience and knowledge. This differs from his father's perspective because he has the experience and knowledge of how to make a fire and other things involving fire. He is able to use his knowledge and experience to teach Jake these things.

38. B: Personification is a figure of speech that gives nonhuman things human like attributes, nature, or characteristics. Therefore, the only sentence out of the choices available that gives a nonhuman thing a human characteristic is choice B. In this sentence, the flames are the nonhuman thing, and they "crept up the corners".

39. A: The best summary of this passage is that a young boy names Jake learns how to gather small pieces of wood to start a fire with his father's guidance and support. He did not teach his father, he was not with friends, and he did not learn it at boy scouts.

40. C: The word "flickering" means wavering or flittering with quick, irregular motions. It is referring to the fire light.

Answers and Explanations for Test #2

1. D: The author's purpose of this selection is to explain how to make cheese crackers. The purpose is not to persuade the reader to make cheese crackers, and it is not to entertain the reader.

2. C: The best summary of this passage is that Mika and her mother follow a recipe to make cheese crackers since her mom has yet to get snacks from the store for Mika to eat.

3. A: According to the recipe, covering the bowl with plastic wrap should be done before the other three answer choice options.

4. B: The items needed to make the crackers are listed under the word "ingredients." Therefore, "ingredients" means the items necessary to make a food or dish.

5. B: Mika's mom fixed her problem of wanting food immediately by giving her an apple as a small snack while they take the time to make the crackers.

6. A: By saying to add the water "one tablespoon at a time," the writer is telling the cook to add the water a little bit at a time or gradually.

7. C: Mika is impatient and complaining about being hungry at first; however, after her mom gives her an apple as a small snack and explains how they can make crackers from scratch, her attitude shifts as she becomes willing to wait and learn.

8. A: Mika reads the cheese cracker recipe because she wants to make cheese crackers.

9. C: A hyperbole is an exaggerated statement that is not meant to be taken literally. While Mika is indeed probably very hungry, she is exaggerating how hungry she is. She is not literally starving.

10. B: Personification is a figure of speech that gives nonhuman things human like attributes, nature, or characteristics. Floorboards cannot creak and moan, so this is an example of personification in the story.

11. D: That's just Sammy's imagination getting out of hand. This phrase tells the reader that Hakeem's mother thinks Sammy makes up things, and she does not trust his judgment.

12. C: Hakeem is not afraid of scary movies, and he laughed when he heard ghost stories by a campfire. This shows that Hakeem is brave and does not get scared easily.

13. B: Hakeem believes Gerard because his brother "does not joke around." Also, Hakeem did not think Gerard was trying to scare him, but rather was trying to warn him. This shows that Gerard is honest.

14. A: At the beginning of the story, Hakeem was very fearful of what he had been told about the museum being haunted. However, as the story progressed, he became more confident as he gained understanding of why strange things were happening. He ended up thoroughly enjoying his experience.

15. A: The small number of lamps and the one flickering bulb overhead gave the idea that the room was not lit well. Because of this, the word dim most likely means "badly lit."

16. D: Hakeem laughed because he found out that what his brother thought were ghosts actually were just creaking floorboards and a flickering bulb. He laughed because there was a logical explanation for the scary parts of the room.

17. B: Appearances can be deceiving. The creaking floorboards and jumping shadows mislead Gerard to think a ghost was in the room. What Gerard thought he saw turned out to be something completely different and safe.

18. C: The last thing that happened in the story out of the answer choices provided was Malcolm walking around like a duck. The county historian gave the class a tour at the beginning of the story. Gerard told Hakeem about the haunted room in the museum at the beginning of the story as well. The light flickered over the mannequin towards the end of the story, but Malcolm did not start walking like a duck until after that had happened.

19. B: Gloria shows goats, is 12-years-old, and lives on her family farm near Austin, Texas.

20. A: The best way to summarize this journal entry is that Manuela recounts her visit to the Texas State Fair where she got to watch her cousin Gloria show her goats.

21. D: The main idea of this journal entry is that being unique can lead to success. Maja, the loud goat, captured the judges' attention due to her differences from the other goats and won.

22. B: Manuela changes throughout the story because at first she thought there was only one way to reach success, but she ended up gaining a new perspective and realized there are many ways to reach success.

23. C: In the story, Gloria, Manuela's cousin, is the only other character that slightly changes since it seemed like she was slightly surprised that Maja did better than Henry since Henry was very quiet and Maja was not. After Maja placed, Gloria's perspective of the judges changed.

24. C: After Manuela's father put coffee in his thermos and before they saw Gloria show her goats, Manuela and her father waited for half-an-hour to park.

25. A: The story says that she got into the fair at almost 8 a.m., which is two hours after 6 a.m.

26. B: A metaphor is a figure of speech where one thing is described as if it were something else to make a comparison. "The squeaky wheel" refers to the loud goat, and "gets the grease" refers to getting attention. Thus, it means that the goat got attention and won due to his vocal behavior.

27. B: Since Henry was quiet and well-behaved, the judges didn't really remember him very much; however, Maja's loud behavior left a very memorable impression on the judges because it stood out from the other goats.

28. D: The squeaky wheel in this story was Maja. Even though she was noisy in the ring, she still won a prize. Perhaps the judges indeed understood "goat"!

29. B: This text is informational since it is an invitation to a party. It lists all the important details an individual would need to know in order to attend the party.

30. C: The purpose of this text is to invite people to a birthday party.

31. A: The author would like a response through a phone call or text message since they listed a number for the receiver of the invitation to reply to.

32. B: Out of the answer choices given, the most logical reason the author wants a response to the invitation is to know how many people they will have to feed and how much food needs to be made. It is unlikely that the author invited too many people to fit into the pool. It is also unlikely that the author is planning a bunch of games since they will be swimming. The author does not need to know how many horses to reserve since it is a pool party.

33. D: The party is a birthday party for Patricio Suarez. This can be determined since it says that Patricio Suarez turns twelve years old.

34. C: Next to "bring," the invitation says "bathing suit." From this, one can infer that swimming will be the main activity at the party.

35. B: This poem is rhymed verse since it has a consistent rhyme scheme. Free verse poems do not follow a specific rhyme or meter. Haiku poems are 3 lines with a syllable pattern of 5-7-5. Limericks are humorous poems with a very specific pattern of AABBA.

36. B: The mother tucks her into bed.

37. A: The best summary of the poem is that a child finds comfort in the loving care of their mother while sick.

38. D: While the author does not enjoy feeling sick, she does value the way her mom cares for her while she is sick.

39. A: A hyperbole is an exaggerated statement that is not meant to be taken literally. Thus, when the author of the poem says that his mom gives him a blanket so she won't freeze, the author would not literally end up frozen without it. The author would just be very cold.

40. C: The author's mother does all of the following except make soup for the narrator when she is sick.

How to Overcome Test Anxiety

Just the thought of taking a test is enough to make most people a little nervous. A test is an important event that can have a long-term impact on your future, so it's important to take it seriously and it's natural to feel anxious about performing well. But just because anxiety is normal, that doesn't mean that it's helpful in test taking, or that you should simply accept it as part of your life. Anxiety can have a variety of effects. These effects can be mild, like making you feel slightly nervous, or severe, like blocking your ability to focus or remember even a simple detail.

If you experience test anxiety—whether severe or mild—it's important to know how to beat it. To discover this, first you need to understand what causes test anxiety.

Causes of Test Anxiety

While we often think of anxiety as an uncontrollable emotional state, it can actually be caused by simple, practical things. One of the most common causes of test anxiety is that a person does not feel adequately prepared for their test. This feeling can be the result of many different issues such as poor study habits or lack of organization, but the most common culprit is time management. Starting to study too late, failing to organize your study time to cover all of the material, or being distracted while you study will mean that you're not well prepared for the test. This may lead to cramming the night before, which will cause you to be physically and mentally exhausted for the test. Poor time management also contributes to feelings of stress, fear, and hopelessness as you realize you are not well prepared but don't know what to do about it.

Other times, test anxiety is not related to your preparation for the test but comes from unresolved fear. This may be a past failure on a test, or poor performance on tests in general. It may come from comparing yourself to others who seem to be performing better or from the stress of living up to expectations. Anxiety may be driven by fears of the future—how failure on this test would affect your educational and career goals. These fears are often completely irrational, but they can still negatively impact your test performance.

Elements of Test Anxiety

As mentioned earlier, test anxiety is considered to be an emotional state, but it has physical and mental components as well. Sometimes you may not even realize that you are suffering from test anxiety until you notice the physical symptoms. These can include trembling hands, rapid heartbeat, sweating, nausea, and tense muscles. Extreme anxiety may lead to fainting or vomiting. Obviously, any of these symptoms can have a negative impact on testing. It is important to recognize them as soon as they begin to occur so that you can address the problem before it damages your performance.

The mental components of test anxiety include trouble focusing and inability to remember learned information. During a test, your mind is on high alert, which can help you recall information and stay focused for an extended period of time. However, anxiety interferes with your mind's natural processes, causing you to blank out, even on the questions you know well. The strain of testing during anxiety makes it difficult to stay focused, especially on a test that may take several hours. Extreme anxiety can take a huge mental toll, making it difficult not only to recall test information but even to understand the test questions or pull your thoughts together.

Effects of Test Anxiety

Test anxiety is like a disease—if left untreated, it will get progressively worse. Anxiety leads to poor performance, and this reinforces the feelings of fear and failure, which in turn lead to poor performances on subsequent tests. It can grow from a mild nervousness to a crippling condition. If allowed to progress, test anxiety can have a big impact on your schooling, and consequently on your future.

Test anxiety can spread to other parts of your life. Anxiety on tests can become anxiety in any stressful situation, and blanking on a test can turn into panicking in a job situation. But fortunately, you don't have to let anxiety rule your testing and determine your grades. There are a number of relatively simple steps you can take to move past anxiety and function normally on a test and in the rest of life.

Physical Steps for Beating Test Anxiety

While test anxiety is a serious problem, the good news is that it can be overcome. It doesn't have to control your ability to think and remember information. While it may take time, you can begin taking steps today to beat anxiety.

Just as your first hint that you may be struggling with anxiety comes from the physical symptoms, the first step to treating it is also physical. Rest is crucial for having a clear, strong mind. If you are tired, it is much easier to give in to anxiety. But if you establish good sleep habits, your body and mind will be ready to perform optimally, without the strain of exhaustion. Additionally, sleeping well helps you to retain information better, so you're more likely to recall the answers when you see the test questions.

Getting good sleep means more than going to bed on time. It's important to allow your brain time to relax. Take study breaks from time to time so it doesn't get overworked, and don't study right before bed. Take time to rest your mind before trying to rest your body, or you may find it difficult to fall asleep.

Along with sleep, other aspects of physical health are important in preparing for a test. Good nutrition is vital for good brain function. Sugary foods and drinks may give a burst of energy but this burst is followed by a crash, both physically and emotionally. Instead, fuel your body with protein and vitamin-rich foods.

Also, drink plenty of water. Dehydration can lead to headaches and exhaustion, especially if your brain is already under stress from the rigors of the test. Particularly if your test is a long one, drink water during the breaks. And if possible, take an energy-boosting snack to eat between sections.

Along with sleep and diet, a third important part of physical health is exercise. Maintaining a steady workout schedule is helpful, but even taking 5-minute study breaks to walk can help get your blood pumping faster and clear your head. Exercise also releases endorphins, which contribute to a positive feeling and can help combat test anxiety.

When you nurture your physical health, you are also contributing to your mental health. If your body is healthy, your mind is much more likely to be healthy as well. So take time to rest, nourish your body with healthy food and water, and get moving as much as possible. Taking these physical steps will make you stronger and more able to take the mental steps necessary to overcome test anxiety.

Mental Steps for Beating Test Anxiety

Working on the mental side of test anxiety can be more challenging, but as with the physical side, there are clear steps you can take to overcome it. As mentioned earlier, test anxiety often stems from lack of preparation, so the obvious solution is to prepare for the test. Effective studying may be the most important weapon you have for beating test anxiety, but you can and should employ several other mental tools to combat fear.

First, boost your confidence by reminding yourself of past success—tests or projects that you aced. If you're putting as much effort into preparing for this test as you did for those, there's no reason you should expect to fail here. Work hard to prepare; then trust your preparation.

Second, surround yourself with encouraging people. It can be helpful to find a study group, but be sure that the people you're around will encourage a positive attitude. If you spend time with others who are anxious or cynical, this will only contribute to your own anxiety. Look for others who are motivated to study hard from a desire to succeed, not from a fear of failure.

Third, reward yourself. A test is physically and mentally tiring, even without anxiety, and it can be helpful to have something to look forward to. Plan an activity following the test, regardless of the outcome, such as going to a movie or getting ice cream.

When you are taking the test, if you find yourself beginning to feel anxious, remind yourself that you know the material. Visualize successfully completing the test. Then take a few deep, relaxing breaths and return to it. Work through the questions carefully but with confidence, knowing that you are capable of succeeding.

Developing a healthy mental approach to test taking will also aid in other areas of life. Test anxiety affects more than just the actual test—it can be damaging to your mental health and even contribute to depression. It's important to beat test anxiety before it becomes a problem for more than testing.

Study Strategy

Being prepared for the test is necessary to combat anxiety, but what does being prepared look like? You may study for hours on end and still not feel prepared. What you need is a strategy for test prep. The next few pages outline our recommended steps to help you plan out and conquer the challenge of preparation.

Step 1: Scope Out the Test

Learn everything you can about the format (multiple choice, essay, etc.) and what will be on the test. Gather any study materials, course outlines, or sample exams that may be available. Not only will this help you to prepare, but knowing what to expect can help to alleviate test anxiety.

Step 2: Map Out the Material

Look through the textbook or study guide and make note of how many chapters or sections it has. Then divide these over the time you have. For example, if a book has 15 chapters and you have five days to study, you need to cover three chapters each day. Even better, if you have the time, leave an extra day at the end for overall review after you have gone through the material in depth.

If time is limited, you may need to prioritize the material. Look through it and make note of which sections you think you already have a good grasp on, and which need review. While you are studying, skim quickly through the familiar sections and take more time on the challenging parts.

Write out your plan so you don't get lost as you go. Having a written plan also helps you feel more in control of the study, so anxiety is less likely to arise from feeling overwhelmed at the amount to cover.

Step 3: Gather Your Tools

Decide what study method works best for you. Do you prefer to highlight in the book as you study and then go back over the highlighted portions? Or do you type out notes of the important information? Or is it helpful to make flashcards that you can carry with you? Assemble the pens, index cards, highlighters, post-it notes, and any other materials you may need so you won't be distracted by getting up to find things while you study.

If you're having a hard time retaining the information or organizing your notes, experiment with different methods. For example, try color-coding by subject with colored pens, highlighters, or post-it notes. If you learn better by hearing, try recording yourself reading your notes so you can listen while in the car, working out, or simply sitting at your desk. Ask a friend to quiz you from your flashcards, or try teaching someone the material to solidify it in your mind.

Step 4: Create Your Environment

It's important to avoid distractions while you study. This includes both the obvious distractions like visitors and the subtle distractions like an uncomfortable chair (or a too-comfortable couch that makes you want to fall asleep). Set up the best study environment possible: good lighting and a comfortable work area. If background music helps you focus, you may want to turn it on, but otherwise keep the room quiet. If you are using a computer to take notes, be sure you don't have any other windows open, especially applications like social media, games, or anything else that could distract you. Silence your phone and turn off notifications. Be sure to keep water close by so you stay hydrated while you study (but avoid unhealthy drinks and snacks).

Also, take into account the best time of day to study. Are you freshest first thing in the morning? Try to set aside some time then to work through the material. Is your mind clearer in the afternoon or evening? Schedule your study session then. Another method is to study at the same time of day that you will take the test, so that your brain gets used to working on the material at that time and will be ready to focus at test time.

Step 5: Study!

Once you have done all the study preparation, it's time to settle into the actual studying. Sit down, take a few moments to settle your mind so you can focus, and begin to follow your study plan. Don't give in to distractions or let yourself procrastinate. This is your time to prepare so you'll be ready to fearlessly approach the test. Make the most of the time and stay focused.

Of course, you don't want to burn out. If you study too long you may find that you're not retaining the information very well. Take regular study breaks. For example, taking five minutes out of every hour to walk briskly, breathing deeply and swinging your arms, can help your mind stay fresh.

As you get to the end of each chapter or section, it's a good idea to do a quick review. Remind yourself of what you learned and work on any difficult parts. When you feel that you've mastered the material, move on to the next part. At the end of your study session, briefly skim through your notes again.

But while review is helpful, cramming last minute is NOT. If at all possible, work ahead so that you won't need to fit all your study into the last day. Cramming overloads your brain with more information than it can process and retain, and your tired mind may struggle to recall even previously learned information when it is overwhelmed with last-minute study. Also, the urgent nature of cramming and the stress placed on your brain contribute to anxiety. You'll be more likely to go to the test feeling unprepared and having trouble thinking clearly.

So don't cram, and don't stay up late before the test, even just to review your notes at a leisurely pace. Your brain needs rest more than it needs to go over the information again. In fact, plan to finish your studies by noon or early afternoon the day before the test. Give your brain the rest of the day to relax or focus on other things, and get a good night's sleep. Then you will be fresh for the test and better able to recall what you've studied.

Step 6: Take a Practice Test

Many courses offer sample tests, either online or in the study materials. This is an excellent resource to check whether you have mastered the material, as well as to prepare for the test format and environment.

Check the test format ahead of time: the number of questions, the type (multiple choice, free response, etc.), and the time limit. Then create a plan for working through them. For example, if you have 30 minutes to take a 60-question test, your limit is 30 seconds per question. Spend less time on the questions you know well so that you can take more time on the difficult ones.

If you have time to take several practice tests, take the first one open book, with no time limit. Work through the questions at your own pace and make sure you fully understand them. Gradually work up to taking a test under test conditions: sit at a desk with all study materials put away and set a timer. Pace yourself to make sure you finish the test with time to spare and go back to check your answers if you have time.

After each test, check your answers. On the questions you missed, be sure you understand why you missed them. Did you misread the question (tests can use tricky wording)? Did you forget the information? Or was it something you hadn't learned? Go back and study any shaky areas that the practice tests reveal.

Taking these tests not only helps with your grade, but also aids in combating test anxiety. If you're already used to the test conditions, you're less likely to worry about it, and working through tests until you're scoring well gives you a confidence boost. Go through the practice tests until you feel comfortable, and then you can go into the test knowing that you're ready for it.

Test Tips

On test day, you should be confident, knowing that you've prepared well and are ready to answer the questions. But aside from preparation, there are several test day strategies you can employ to maximize your performance.

First, as stated before, get a good night's sleep the night before the test (and for several nights before that, if possible). Go into the test with a fresh, alert mind rather than staying up late to study.

Try not to change too much about your normal routine on the day of the test. It's important to eat a nutritious breakfast, but if you normally don't eat breakfast at all, consider eating just a protein bar. If you're a coffee drinker, go ahead and have your normal coffee. Just make sure you time it so that the caffeine doesn't wear off right in the middle of your test. Avoid sugary beverages, and drink enough water to stay hydrated but not so much that you need a restroom break 10 minutes into the test. If your test isn't first thing in the morning, consider going for a walk or doing a light workout before the test to get your blood flowing.

Allow yourself enough time to get ready, and leave for the test with plenty of time to spare so you won't have the anxiety of scrambling to arrive in time. Another reason to be early is to select a good seat. It's helpful to sit away from doors and windows, which can be distracting. Find a good seat, get out your supplies, and settle your mind before the test begins.

When the test begins, start by going over the instructions carefully, even if you already know what to expect. Make sure you avoid any careless mistakes by following the directions.

Then begin working through the questions, pacing yourself as you've practiced. If you're not sure on an answer, don't spend too much time on it, and don't let it shake your confidence. Either skip it and come back later, or eliminate as many wrong answers as possible and guess among the remaining ones. Don't dwell on these questions as you continue—put them out of your mind and focus on what lies ahead.

Be sure to read all of the answer choices, even if you're sure the first one is the right answer. Sometimes you'll find a better one if you keep reading. But don't second-guess yourself if you do immediately know the answer. Your gut instinct is usually right. Don't let test anxiety rob you of the information you know.

If you have time at the end of the test (and if the test format allows), go back and review your answers. Be cautious about changing any, since your first instinct tends to be correct, but make sure you didn't misread any of the questions or accidentally mark the wrong answer choice. Look over any you skipped and make an educated guess.

At the end, leave the test feeling confident. You've done your best, so don't waste time worrying about your performance or wishing you could change anything. Instead, celebrate the successful completion of this test. And finally, use this test to learn how to deal with anxiety even better next time.

Review Video: Test Anxiety
Visit mometrix.com/academy and enter code: 100340

Important Qualification

Not all anxiety is created equal. If your test anxiety is causing major issues in your life beyond the classroom or testing center, or if you are experiencing troubling physical symptoms related to your anxiety, it may be a sign of a serious physiological or psychological condition. If this sounds like your situation, we strongly encourage you to seek professional help.

Online Resources

Due to our efforts to try to keep this book to a manageable length, we've created a link that will give you access to all of your online resources:

mometrix.com/resources719/flg3elarwb

It's Your Moment, Let's Celebrate It!

Share your story @mometrixtestpreparation